Cambridge Elements

Elements in the Philosophy of Physics
edited by
James Owen Weatherall
University of California, Irvine

CLASSICAL AND QUANTUM PHASE SPACE MECHANICS

Karim Pierre Yves Thébault
University of Bristol

Shaftesbury Road, Cambridge CB2 8EA, United Kingdom

One Liberty Plaza, 20th Floor, New York, NY 10006, USA

477 Williamstown Road, Port Melbourne, VIC 3207, Australia

314–321, 3rd Floor, Plot 3, Splendor Forum, Jasola District Centre, New Delhi – 110025, India

103 Penang Road, #05–06/07, Visioncrest Commercial, Singapore 238467

Cambridge University Press is part of Cambridge University Press & Assessment, a department of the University of Cambridge.

We share the University's mission to contribute to society through the pursuit of education, learning and research at the highest international levels of excellence.

www.cambridge.org
Information on this title: www.cambridge.org/9781009598477

DOI: 10.1017/9781009352055

© Karim Pierre Yves Thébault 2026

This publication is in copyright. Subject to statutory exception and to the provisions of relevant collective licensing agreements, no reproduction of any part may take place without the written permission of Cambridge University Press & Assessment.

When citing this work, please include a reference to the DOI 10.1017/9781009352055

First published 2026

A catalogue record for this publication is available from the British Library

ISBN 978-1-009-59847-7 Hardback
ISBN 978-1-009-35203-1 Paperback
ISSN 2632-413X (online)
ISSN 2632-4121 (print)

Cambridge University Press & Assessment has no responsibility for the persistence or accuracy of URLs for external or third-party internet websites referred to in this publication and does not guarantee that any content on such websites is, or will remain, accurate or appropriate.

For EU product safety concerns, contact us at Calle de José Abascal, 56, 1°, 28003 Madrid, Spain, or email eugpsr@cambridge.org

Classical and Quantum Phase Space Mechanics

Elements in the Philosophy of Physics

DOI: 10.1017/9781009352055
First published online: January 2026

Karim Pierre Yves Thébault
University of Bristol

Author for correspondence: Karim Pierre Yves Thébault, karim.thebault@bristol.ac.uk

Abstract: This Element explores the formal and conceptual foundations of phase space formulations of classical and quantum mechanics. It provides an overview of the core mathematical and physical content of Hamiltonian mechanics, stochastic phase space mechanics, contact Hamiltonian mechanics, and open and closed quantum mechanics on phase space. The formal material is unified via three interpretative themes relating to structured possibility spaces, Liouville's theorem and its failure, and the classical and quantum notions of open and closed systems. This Element is intended for researchers and graduate students in the philosophy and foundations of physics with an interest in the conceptual foundations of physical theory.

Keywords: phase space, representational spaces, geometric mechanics, open quantum systems, representational capacities

© Karim Pierre Yves Thébault 2026

ISBNs: 9781009598477 (HB), 9781009352031 (PB), 9781009352055 (OC)
ISSNs: 2632-413X (online), 2632-4121 (print)

Contents

1	Introduction	1
2	Elements of Differential Geometry	10
3	Symplectic Geometry and Phase Space Mechanics	18
4	Probability and Statistical Phase Space Mechanics	27
5	Dissipation and Contact Phase Space Mechanics	39
6	Quasi-Probability and Quantum Phase Space Mechanics	47
7	Decoherence and Open Quantum Phase Space Mechanics	62
8	Representation and Possibility	73
	References	80

1 Introduction
1.1 The Third Revolution

Mechanics is not matter in motion. It is geometric structure in possibility. For more than a century, the principal mode of representation for mechanical theory has been via higher dimensional possibility spaces. Primary amongst these are *phase spaces*. This Element is about the *structure* of these spaces and the manner in which this structure affords *representations* of mechanical systems. Our intention is to set out the core mathematical and physical content of classical and quantum phase space mechanics as a staging post for future foundational investigation. Whilst we confine ourselves to phase space representations in finite dimensions, the content of this Element is relevant to the foundations of essentially all areas of modern physics. Each of classical mechanics, statistical mechanics, quantum theory, and general relativity admits phase space formulations and, as such, foundational questions from each of these areas can be reformulated in phase space terms. Moreover, the phase space representation is perhaps uniquely positioned to provide formal means to explore the connection *between* physical theories, most significantly the complex of relationships between open and closed, and statistical and quantum theories which is one of the primary motivation for our study.

From a more historical perspective, it is worth remarking that the transition to the study of physical theory in terms of phase spaces can be understood to mark *third* revolutionary change in physical theory, foundationally as important and almost coincident with the quantum and relativity revolutions, but vastly less studied by historians and philosophers of science. This is the transformation from the *quantitive* to the *qualitative* methods in the study of dynamical systems that ran from the late nineteenth century to the mid twentieth century and had as its crowning achievement the celebrated Kolmogorov–Arnold–Moser (KAM) theorem which establishes, under certain conditions, the persistence under small perturbations of quasi-periodic motions in 'most' initial states of a Hamiltonian dynamical systems (Arnold, Kozlov, & Neishtadt, 2006, §6.3).

The quantitive to qualitative revolution was initiated by a series of results concerning the stability of the solar system in the last decade of the nineteenth century by Henri Poincaré and brought together in his monumental *Les Méthodes Nouvelles de la Mécanique Céleste* (New Methods of Celestial Mechanics) published in three volumes between 1892 and 1899. The essence of Poincaré's qualitative approach was a set of new *methods* for the study of features of *sets of solutions* to a mechanical problem in terms of properties of flows on phase spaces. As noted by Abraham and Marsden in the introduction to their textbook, this qualitative approach then immediately suggests a connection between *physical properties* such as stability, and the *geometric structure* of phase space:

> [Poincaré] visualised a dynamical system as a field of vectors on a phase space, in which a solution is a smooth curve tangent at each of its points to the vector at that point. The qualitative theory is based on geometric properties of the *phase portrait*: the family of solution curves, which fill up the entire phase space. For questions such as stability, it is necessary to study the entire phase portrait including the behaviour for all values of the time parameter. Thus it was essential to consider the entire phase space at once as a geometric object... [The] special geometric structure pertaining to the occurrence of phase variables in canonical conjugate pairs [is] a *symplectic structure*. (Abraham & Marsden, 1980, p.xviii)

One of the key stepping stones to Poincaré's stability results was his demonstration of the generic existence of an integral invariant, equivalent to symplectic volume form, under the dynamics (Goroff, 1993, p. 179). This result was earlier proved by both Liouville (1838) and Boltzmann (1871) and is now known as *Liouville's theorem*. It is the first and arguably most basic result of qualitative mechanics. Liouville's theorem and its failure will be one of the three interconnected themes that run throughout this Element.

The other two themes are, first, more generally, the conceptualisation of phase spaces as structured possibility spaces and, second, more specifically, the connection between the notions of 'open' and 'closed' mechanical systems, dissipation and decoherence, and the idea of probability and quasi-probability flows on phase spaces as incompressible fluid flows. Whilst the first topic has been subject to a limited discussion in the philosophical literature, the second is a novel intervention, and, as such this Element can be understood, in part, as a short research monograph setting out a novel interpretative stance on these topics.

Our main focus is didactic not dialectic. This Element is primarily intended for researchers and graduate students in the philosophy and foundations of physics with an interest in the conceptual foundations of phase space formulations of mechanics. As such, our primary goal is a pedagogical and expository one. An array of formal and conceptual machinery for the analysis of phase space mechanics is introduced and it is hoped that a suitable platform for further studies and research on the topic has been provided.

The formal material presented here is designed to be largely self-contained. The first section focuses upon introducing some key geometric ideas clearly and with a degree of rigour. We will not attempt to offer a comprehensive introduction to differential geometry but rather seek to build up the key conceptual tools assuming some familiarity with manifolds and maps. When we draw on key concepts from topology and analysis we will provide reference to good discussions rather than formal definitions. This will allow the reader a degree of formal foundation from which to understand what it means to formulate the Hamiltonian formulation of classical mechanics in terms of symplectic geometry. Similarly, later we will introduce some basic concepts from measure theory such that the reader can situate the use of probability density functions in stochastic phase space formulations of mechanics in a suitably rigorous mathematical context without requiring an entire course in analysis.

Our goal is to provide the reader with both physical and mathematical intuitions for the structure of classical and quantum phase space representations in finite dimensions. To that end, we will return in each context to the specific example of simple harmonic motion. Each section will include the explicit study of this system and we invite the reader to run through the straightforward calculations themselves. We will largely proceed without step-by-step proofs but with provide reference to relevant results in the literature. Each section concludes with a list of topics for future study with an aim of both establishing connections to existing literature and highlighting issues that are suitable topic for creative graduate work on the topic.

1.2 Modal Structure and Representation

Before we commence our project proper, it will prove useful to provide some ancillary philosophical motivation in terms of the exploration the conceptual foundations of *possibility spaces* and their role in the representation of *modal structure*. The concept of modal structure has been much discussed in the context of Ontic Structural Realism (Berenstain & Ladyman, 2011; Ladyman, 1998, 2024; Ladyman & Lorenzetti, 2023; Ladyman & Ross, 2007). In that context, it is understood as a general term that subsumes causal structure, mechanisms, nomological structure, probabilistic and statistical structures. Here we will always and only use the term in a much more restrictive sense as relating to the interpretation of mathematical structures on a possibility space. Such a notion requires no consideration of the metaphysics of causation, laws, mechanisms, or dispositions – a metaphysics which has little, if any, relevance to scientific practice in the context of phase space mechanics (and arguably more widely).

The idea of explicitly interpreting phase spaces as possibility spaces can be found in Rickles (2007). In particular, Rickles suggests that we should understand geometric spaces as being used to represent the 'possibility structures' of theories. On this account, the models given by a space and geometric structure function as 'possibility spaces' in sense that one starts with a set of possibilities, as represented by the 'bare' manifold, and then imposes a geometrical structure on the manifold to give space that represents relationships between these possibilities (Rickles, 2007, p.10).

A further idea that proves useful here is the distinction between *material* and *formal* modes as introduced by Ladyman and Ross (2007) following Carnap (1934), cf. Ladyman & Thebault (2024). The idea is very simple yet deceptively powerful. Concepts and terms are used in the *material mode* when applied to *concrete systems*, and in the *formal mode* when applied to *representations*, that is, linguistic or mathematical structures. We thus have that to discuss a physical system X in the material mode is to make an ontological claim about the properties of X. To discuss X in the formal mode is to refer to the representations (linguistic or mathematical structures) of X. If X is a possible state of the world in material mode, then, in the formal mode, we can think then think of any given phase space point as a representation of such a possibility.

Next, following Weatherall (2018) and Fletcher (2020), we can define the *representational capacities* of a scientific model as *the states of affairs that the model may be used to represent well*. The representational capacities of a possibility space are then understood to be the *structured set* of *possible* states of affairs that the space may be used to represent well. The structures imposed upon this space then correspond to constraints or prescriptions with regard to the space's representational capabilities. For example, Liouville's theorem tells us that the possible states of affairs that can be repented by a Hamiltonian phase space must be represented as occupying a stable volume of possibility space over time.

One then arrives at the immediate and highly challenging question: *what is the material mode correlate of the constraints or prescriptions with regard to a space's representational capabilities*? In other words, if we consider the part of the model that encodes how the possibilities it can represent relate to each other, can we still think of there being a *material mode* counterpart to which it corresponds. Let us call this material mode counterpart *modal structure*.

This idea brings to mind the trailblazing discussion of Saunders (1993). Saunders considers what Post (1971) had earlier called the *generalized principle of correspondence*: what is taken over from preceding theories is not only those laws and experimental facts which are well-confirmed, but also 'patterns' and 'internal connections'. He then suggests that a strong candidate for such internal connections are structures such as the Poisson bracket in phase space formalism of classical mechanics which was, of course, 'deformed' through theory change into the commutator of quantum theory. Saunders emphasises the historical heuristic fruitfulness of focusing upon structures such as the Poisson bracket, and pivotally their *heuristic plasticity*.

This idea is further emphasised by French (2011), who indicates that precisely these structures are the dynamical structures that an Ontic Structural Realists should be realists about cf. Ladyman (1998, 2023). We thus have a straightforward response to our question: the aspect of a phase space model that encodes how the possibilities it can represent relate to each other represents ontic modal structure and such structure can ontology promoted to a 'thing' along the lines discussed by Berenstain and Ladyman (2011) cf. Thébault (2016). One major attractive feature of such a view of ontic structural realist approach to phase space is that it allows us to make sense of the truth-makers for highly significant modal claims regarding physical systems. One of the features of the world that the truth of modal claims, such as the stability of the solar system, depends upon is the existence of ontic modal structure that is represented by (is the material model correlate of) the satisfaction of Liouville's theorem. The theorem encodes real structure relating to how possibilities relate to each.

Such a metaphysically thick approach to modal structure may not, however, sit well with all. A healthy, Humean scepticism warns us to be wary of interpreting modal talk metaphysically. It would, however, strain the bonds of philosophical naturalism to seek to diminish the scientific explanatory role of possibility space structure by attempting to either reduce away or eliminate its modal character cf. Lyon and Colyvan (2008). After all, if the qualitative revolution in mechanics has given us anything it is an ability to make precise *modal claims* regarding physical systems based upon geometric features of phase spaces.

This sentiment against *both* realism and eliminativism regarding modal structure brings to mind a general strategy for responding to tricky philosophical 'placement' problems: *expressivism*. Following Price (2008), we can understand such problems to occur when we have trouble locating the 'placement' of a particular class of things that feature in our vocabulary without our ontology. For example, moral or causal facts. The standard expressivist response to such problems, which Price traces back to Hume, is to argue that the placement issue originates from a category error. Our tendency to seek to 'place' moral or causal facts within the world reflects a mistaken understanding of the function of causal or moral vocabulary within our discourse. We note that this language is not in the business of 'describing reality' and offer some other positive account of what functional role this vocabulary plays in our linguistic lives.

What prospect is there for offering an expressivist account of the modal structure of possibility spaces that avoids the placement problem? The most detailed discussion of the idea of a *modal expressivism* can be found in the extended exegeses of the ideas of Wilfred Sellars due to Brandom (2015) and is encapsulated within what Brandom calls the *modal Kant-Sellars thesis* (see in particular p. 26 & p.212). The thesis can be expressed in terms of a claim articulated in three stages. First, that there is a *relation* between the *use* of modal vocabulary and the *use* of empirical descriptive vocabulary. Second, that this relation is one of *pragmatic dependence* in which the use of modal vocabulary can be *elaborated* from the use of descriptive vocabulary. Third, that this elaboration *does no more* than make implicit features of the descriptive vocabulary explicit. According to the thesis 'in being able to use ordinary empirical descriptive vocabulary, one already knows how to do everything that one needs to know how to do, in principle, to use alethic modal vocabulary – in particular subjunctive conditionals' (p.26). Thus, '[m]odal expressivism tells us that modal vocabulary makes explicit normatively significant relations of subjunctively robust material consequence and incompatibility among claimable (hence propositional) contents' (p.212).

To what extent can we appeal to modal expressivism in the context of the modal structure of possibility spaces? The first and most basic challenge is to recover the basic modal notions that Sellars and Brandom are concerned with. This is most straightforward in the case of the core 'alethic' modal vocabulary of natural language: necessity, possibility, impossibility, and contingency. In a possibility space model, what is necessary holds of all points in the state space; what is possible holds of at least one point in the state space; what is impossible holds of no points in the state space; and what is contingent holds of some but not all points in the phase space. Next, and also fairly straightforward, are the relations of concepts of material consequence and incompatibility. For Brandom these are normatively significant relations *made explicit* by our ordinary language modal vocabulary. In a possibility space representation, these relations can be framed via reference to generic properties that constrain the dynamics to surfaces in possibility space. Most significantly surfaces of constant value in some integral of motion (tantalisingly Brandom even makes reference to Noether's theorem but draws the connection only to laws rather than possibility space constraints, ibid. p.196).

The modal structure that can be encoded in a possibility space is, however, immeasurably richer than the modal vocabulary of natural language. There is much more than can be said about the structure of possibility in a possibility space representation than in our ordinary modal talk. We might thus understand, geometric and measure theoretic tools to provide us with *novel modal concepts* that build upon the intuitive idea of *structured relations between possibilities*. This is precisely the function notions such as volume of possibility space or dynamical stability are designed to play.

Significantly, these expanded modal concepts are such that it is not obvious how one would explicate them from our ordinary empirical descriptive vocabulary of quantities in space and time. We thus find an interesting tension with the third stage of articulation of Brandom's modal Kant-Sellars thesis. Plausibly, it might *not* be true that in being able to use ordinary empirical descriptive vocabulary, one already knows how to do everything that one needs to know how to do, in principle, to use modal vocabulary. Rather, one might run the pragmatic dependence the other way round. The novel modal vocabulary that possibility space representations afford us with equip us with *new ways of expanding our empirical descriptive vocabulary*. One can might thus understand the modal expressivism motivated by the structure of possibility spaces as a more fluid kind than Brandom describes. Modal vocabulary still has a pragmatic dependence on descriptive vocabulary, in this case the descriptions of states of the world encoded in points in possibility spaces, but it can do much more than simply make explicit already acquired functions of that vocabulary. It can equipped us with new expressive tools.

An alternative interpretation, more in keeping with Brandom's approach, would to frame the novelty of the relevant modal concepts as being with respect to the natural vs. scientific language rather than the empirical descriptive vocabulary per se. The idea would be to seek to preserve the third stage of the modal expressivist account and insist that modal language *can only* make implicit features of the descriptive vocabulary explicit. In this context, it is descriptive features of *scientific language*, not contained in ordinary descriptive language, that are made explicit via the modal structure of phase space. Thus, the modal concepts that the structure of phase space equips us with are novel with respect to ordinary descriptive language, and the ordinary modal concepts implicitly contained therein, but are not genuinely novel with respect to scientific descriptive language. Whilst providing such an account of modal structure of phase spaces would fit better with Brandom's modal Kant-Sellars thesis, it appears to require a rather sophisticated meta-semantic account of how the process of 'making explicit' functions in the scientific context. In particular, a meta-semantic account how scientific modal concepts might be explicated from a descriptive vocabulary that lacks, for example, the inherently modal concept of phase space structure. In either case, there is an interesting project of applying the ideas of modal expressivism to scientific language in general and phase space mechanics in particular.

We will return to the articulation of modal expressivist ideas in context of the specific formal features of phase space representations of classical and quantum mechanics in Section 8. We invite the reader to keep idea of *modal structure of possibility spaces* in mind when navigating the mathematical and physical material that follows.

1.3 Section Summaries

The remainder of this Element consists of seven sections. In Section 2 we provide a skeleton overview of key ideas from differential geometry. Most significantly we will introduce the notion of a *two-form* as a geometric means of equipping a phase space with an orientated volume and the *Lie derivative* as a special kind of derivative operator. The Lie derivative allows us to define how a geometric object, such as a function or a two-form, changes along a particular set of directions in a phase space, corresponding to a *vector field*. The directions picked out by a vector field are directly analogous to flow lines in a fluid and thus a Lie derivative can tell us how a geometric object changes under a *flow* associated with any vector field.

Section 3 then introduces the formalisation of phase space in terms of symplectic manifolds. These are even-dimensional manifolds equipped with *symplectic two-forms*. Hamilton's equations of motion are then defined simply by the special Hamilton vector field associated to the Hamiltonian function by the symplectic two-form. Dynamics is a flow on phase space. The famous result of Liouville (and Poincaré) is then simply that for any Hamiltonian system, the Lie derivative of the symplectic two-form along the flow associated with the Hamiltonian function is zero. The dynamics preserves the volume form. This is a *qualitative* result that can be stated without reference to any coordinate system. The structure of a Hamiltonian theory in the symplectic representation is encoded in intrinsic geometric facts invariant under the class of transformations called *symplectomorphisms*.

Section 4 introduces a little more mathematical machinery to allow us to discuss *measures* on phase space via the integration of *probability density functions*. We then show how these objects can be combined with the symplectic version of Hamiltonian mechanics in order to define a set of stochastic phase space models that provide a perspicacious formulation of classical statistical mechanical theory. In this context, Liouville's theorem has a natural presentation in terms of the incompressibility of a probability 'fluid' – which admits no local sources or sinks – and is formally equivalent to statement that the total derivative of the probability density is always vanishing in a stochastic Hamiltonian system. A further important result that can be derived in this formalism *under restricted circumstances* is a classical stochastic version of the Ehrenfest equations in which the first moments of position and momentum obey Newton's first two laws of motion. This provides a simple and direct means to connect stochastic and deterministic models and, moreover, a precise language to understand divergence from the Ehrenfest equations in stochastic models that is also found in quantum theories.

Section 5 considers the geometric formalism for the study of open classical systems that display dissipative behaviour. Our analysis will bring in the tools of contact geometry which are a natural extension of symplectic geometry and allow us to formulate mechanics in odd dimensional phase spaces. Such phase spaces are uniquely suited to the representation of dissipative systems since they provide possibility space models of systems that are mechanically non-conservative, such as an oscillator with a velocity-dependent damping factor. Moreover, contact geometry provides us with a set of geometric models which provide phase representations with structure beyond that encoded in Liouville's theorem. We are able to represent phase space dynamics with compression (or expansion) of the volume form under the contact Hamiltonian flow. This is to represent structured sets of possibilities which occupy a shrinking (or expanding) volume of possibility space over time.

Section 6 introduces the phase space formulation of quantum mechanics focusing on the Wigner function. We first consider some formal ideas relating to the generalisation from a probability density function to a *quasi-probability density function* and some subtle features of the finite signed measure that is induced by such functions. We next build up the quantum phase formalism step by step noting the crucial differences with the stochastic phase space theory in terms of the negativity and non-localisability of the Wigner quasi-probability density function. We then return to our theme of Liouville's theorem and its failure by showing how the local *compressibility* of the quasi-probability density is directly connected to the structure of the Moyal bracket that equips the quantum phase space observables, the *Weyl symbols*, with a non-commutative structure. Finally, we demonstrate the sense in which the Ehrenfest-type relations for the first moments in the quantum phase space formalism correspond to those derived in the context of the stochastic theory.

Section 7 considers the quantum phase space representation of open quantum systems. Such systems are generically represented as having non-unitary dynamics and provide the basis for the study of the phenomena of decoherence. We start with a final piece of mathematics based upon Fourier transforms that leads to the formal idea of a *Gaussian smoothing*. We then consider the general formal structure of an open quantum systems and the relationship between non-unitarity and probability conservation. The successive discussions then introduce the three most important classes of open quantum system master equations the *Lindblad equation*, the *Caldeira-Leggett* equation, and the *Joos-Zeh* equation. The latter two equations are considered in their quantum phase space form. This analysis allows us to demonstrate the formal connections to classical damping via Ehrenfest relations in the case of the Caldeira-Leggett equation and to decoherence and Wigner positivity via Gaussian smoothing in the case of the Joos-Zeh master equation.

The final Section 8 then returns to our theme of representation and possibility and provides an interpretative summary of our results and their implications for the ideas of representational capacity and modal structure.

2 Elements of Differential Geometry

Our main goal in this section is to introduce the idea of *differential forms* together with the four basic operations on differential forms that define the theory of exterior calculus. These are the *wedge product*, $\wedge$, *interior product*, ι, *exterior derivative*, d, and *Lie derivative*, $\mathcal{L}$. We will follow Olver (2000), Arnol'd (2013), and Holm (2011), supplemented by Abraham and Marsden (1980). Additional sources are noted where relevant. We will assume basic concepts from differential geometry such the definition of a differential manifold. The Einstein summation convention is used throughout.

We start by recapping the idea a of *vector field* and *flow* on a manifold. When combined with the language of differential forms this will allow us to provide a fully geometric rendering of phase space mechanics. A vector field, X, on a manifold, M, assigns a tangent vector $X_{|x} \in TM_{|x}$ to each point $x \in M$. In local coordinates a vector field has the form:

$$X_{|x} = X^i(x)\frac{\partial}{\partial x^i} \tag{2.1}$$

where each $X^i(x)$ is a smooth function of x. In what follows we will often write a vector fields simply as $X = X^i \partial_i$ for short. We will write the space of vector fields on a manifold $\mathfrak{X}(M)$. Formally, the space of vector fields on a manifold can also be defined in terms of *smooth sections of the tangent bundle TM* (Abraham & Marsden, 1980).

An integral curve of a vector field is a smooth parametrised curve $x = \phi(\epsilon)$ whose tangent vector $\dot\phi$ at any point, x, coincides with the value of X, so we have:

$$\dot\phi(\epsilon) = X_{|\phi(\epsilon)} \tag{2.2}$$

If we visualise a vector field as an array of arrows on a manifold, then the integral curves are the curves that 'thread' the arrows such that at any point the curve is tangent to the arrow at that point. The parametrised maximal integral curve passing thought $x \in M$ is the flow generated by X which we will write as $\Phi(\epsilon,x)$. The flow generated by a vector field is equivalent to the local group action of the Lie group $\mathbb{R}$ on that manifold. The vector field is then the infinitesimal generator of the group action since the Taylor expansion takes the form:

$$\Phi(\epsilon,x) = x + \epsilon X^1(x) + O(\epsilon^2) \tag{2.3}$$

We can express the flow in terms of the exponentiation of the vector field as:

$$\exp(\epsilon X)x \equiv \Phi(\epsilon,x) \tag{2.4}$$

The property that X is tangent to $\Phi(\epsilon,x)$ for fixed x,

$$\frac{d}{d\epsilon}\Phi(\epsilon,x) = X_{|\Phi(\epsilon,x)} \tag{2.5}$$

can thus be written as:

$$\frac{d}{d\epsilon}\exp(\epsilon X)x = X_{|\exp(\epsilon X)x} \tag{2.6}$$

This way of thinking about the flows in terms of exponentiation will prove crucial for the definition of the fourth operation on differential forms, the Lie derivative. Before we get to that point, let us first introduce the idea of forms itself.

We will focus on giving simple and intuitive definitions. A more formal and concise approach is taken in the following box. In the most general sense, differential forms are a special type of tensors on manifolds. They have the property that they are anti-symmetric under exchange of any pair of indices. Differential forms are the crucial formal object that allow for the standard integral theorems, such as those due to Gauss and Stokes, to be generalised to manifolds of arbitrary dimensions. They are also the central object that allow for the geometrisation of Hamiltonian mechanics. Like tensors in general, differential forms have a *rank*. Intuitively, we can think of this rank as the number of independent dimensions that can be simultaneously associated with a magnitude by the tensor. For our purposes it will be important to understand the formal definition of differential forms of rank 0, 1 and 2. These intuitively correspond a specific type of generalisations of functions, vectors, and matrices respectively.

A rank-0 differential form, or 0-form, on a manifold M is just a smooth real valued function $f: M \to \mathbb{R}$. The differential of the function df at a point $x \in M$ is a linear map, $df(x) : T_xM \to \mathbb{R}$, from the tangent space T_xM of M at x to the real numbers. If we write a local coordinate basis of the tangent space as

$\partial/\partial^j, j = 1, \ldots n$, then a dual basis can be written as a local coordinate basis as $dx, k = 1 \ldots n$. The differential of a function is then written as:

$$df = \frac{\partial f}{\partial x^k} dx^k \tag{2.7}$$

A differential 1-form then has a local coordinate expression in terms of linear combinations of differentials of the coordinates:

$$\theta = f_1(x)dx^1 + \ldots + f_n(x)dx^n \tag{2.8}$$

As such, the space of 1-forms at a point $x \in M$ is just the space of linear functions on the tangent space $TM_{|x}$, This is, by definition, the cotangent space $T^*M_{|x}$, or dual vector space to the tangent space at x. A 1-form on a manifold M is then a smooth section of the cotangent bundle T^*M. Geometrically we can understand a 1-form as defining an orientated line segment.

In order to define the next rank of differential form, the 2-form, it is convenient to introduce the first of our four operations of exterior calculus. This is the *wedge product*, $\wedge$. Its most basic operation is the multiplication of two 1-forms in order to construct a 2-form, that is, it is such that $\omega = \theta_1 \wedge \theta_2$ is a 2-form. In a local 1-form basis $dx^j, j = 1 \ldots n$ we have that:

$$\omega = f_{ij} dx^i \wedge dx^j \tag{2.9}$$

where the sum over repeated indices is ordered so that it is taken for all i,j satisfying $i < j$. The local coordinate expression for a 2-form on $\mathbb{R}^3$ is thus:

$$\omega = f(x,y,z)dy \wedge dz + g(x,y,z)dz \wedge dx + h(x,y,z)dx \wedge dy \tag{2.10}$$

Geometrically we can understand the wedge product as allowing us to compose orientated line segments (1-forms) to construct orientated surface elements (2-forms), then orientated volume elements (3-forms), and so on for arbitrary dimensions (rank of form). That these elements are orientated is equivalent to the fact that the wedge product is anti-symmetric under exchange of indices and so we have that $dx^j \wedge dy^k = -dx^k \wedge dx^j$. See Figure 1 for illustration.

Formally, the anti-symmetry is implied by the fact that the wedge product is the multiplication operation of alternating algebra, which by definition, means that we have that $\theta \wedge \theta = 0$ which implies $\theta_1 \wedge \theta_2 = -\theta_2 \wedge \theta_1$. The interpretation 2-form as an orientated surface between two 1-forms obviously matches with the property that the orientated area of a 1-form with itself is zero. If we consider a two form ω acting on a pair of vectors X and Y then the alternating property is that $\omega(X,Y) = -\omega(Y,X)$ and $\omega(X,X) = 0$ which is the property of *skew-symmetry*. See the following box for more details.

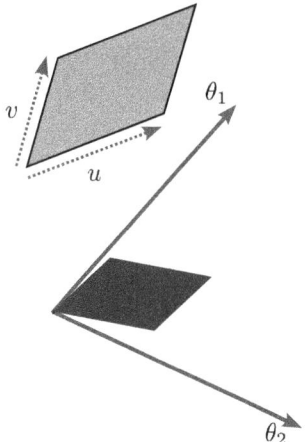

Figure 1 Geometric illustration of 2-form as an orientated area element: $\theta_1 \wedge \theta_2(u,v) = \theta_1(u)\theta_2(v) - \theta_1(v)\theta_2(u) = -\theta_2 \wedge \theta_1(u,v)$.

BOX 1 DIFFERENTIAL k-FORMS AND THE WEDGE PRODUCT

Let M by a smooth manifold and $TM_{|x}$ its tangent space at x. The space $\wedge_k T^*M_{|x}$ of differential k-forms at x is the set of all k-linear alternating functions:

$$\alpha : TM_{|x} \times \ldots \times TM_{|x} \to \mathbb{R} \tag{2.11}$$

A smooth differential k-form α on M is then the collection of smoothly varying alternating k-linear maps $\alpha_{|x} \in \wedge_k T^*M_{|x}$ where we require that the evaluation of the k-form on k smooth vector fields is a smooth real function of x. (Olver, 2000, p. 54)

Differential k-forms on a manifold $\alpha \in \Omega^k(M)$ form an exterior algebra. The wedge product is as an associative, bilinear, anticomputative map that is the product operation on the exterior algebra of differential forms. The wedge product is defined such that if $\alpha \in \Omega^k(M)$ and $\beta \in \Omega^l(M)$ for $k,l = 0\ldots n$ then $\alpha \wedge \beta \in \Omega^{k+l}(M)$ where the explicit form of the $\wedge$ operation can be defined in terms of the tensor product operation as

$$\alpha \wedge \beta = \frac{(k+l)!}{k!l!} A(\alpha \otimes \beta) \tag{2.12}$$

where A is the alternating map. (Abraham & Marsden, 1980, §2.3-4).

The second operation on differential forms is the *interior product*, ι. The interior product is also called the contraction and allows us to compose a differential form with a vector field such that we lower the rank of the form in question. For our purposes the most important application of the interior product is the contraction of a 2-form with a vector field to give a 1-form. In components, the explicit form of the product can be written:

$$\iota_X \omega = \iota_X(f_{jk} dx^j \wedge dx^k) = X^i f_{ij} dx^j \tag{2.13}$$

In two dimensions, the contraction of a vector field, $X = X^j \partial_j = X^1 \partial_1 + X^2 \partial_2$, with a 2-form, $\omega = f_{ij} dx^i \wedge dx^j$ then takes the simple form:

$$\iota_X \omega = X^1 f_{12} dx^2 + X^2 f_{21} dx^1 \tag{2.14}$$

We have thus combined a 2-form with a vector field in order to product a 1-form. The contraction of a 2-form always yields a 1-form (or zero). Later we will find that Hamilton's equations can be expressed in terms of the contraction of a canonical 2-form on phase space.

The contraction of a 1-form is then defined by the interior product of a 1-form with a vector field, which gives us a 0-form. As already noted, a 0-form is just a function. The contraction of a 0-form is always zero, so $\iota_X f = 0$. The interior product of a vector field with a 1-form is equivalent to the dot product between a covariant and contravariant vectors:

$$\iota_X \theta = \iota_X(f_k dx^k) = f_k \delta_j^k X^j = f_j X^j = \mathbf{f} \cdot \mathbf{X} \tag{2.15}$$

where the indices k, j indicate vector components and we assume the Einstein summation convention.

The third operation on differential forms is the is the *exterior derivative*, d. The exterior derivative is the unique family of mappings that raise the rank of a differential form. In this sense it can be thought of the opposite or dual operation to the interior derivative. The exterior product is a linear, local operator and is such that $d^2 = 0$. The exterior derivative of a 0-form is a 1-form and the exterior derivative of a 1-form is a 2-form, and so on. We have already given the formula for the exterior derivative of a 0-form in terms of the expression for the differential of a function Equation (2.7). The exterior derivative of a 1-form is given in coordinates by the expression:

$$d\theta = d(f_i dx^i) = \frac{\partial f_i}{\partial x^k} dx^k \wedge dx^i = df_i \wedge dx^i \tag{2.16}$$

The class of 2-forms, which are such that they can be written as the exterior derivative of a one form, $\omega = d\theta$, are called *exact*. A two form that is such that $d\omega = 0$ is called closed. Since $d^2 = 0$ we have that all exact 2-forms are necessarily closed.

The exterior product allows us to express the following attractive generalisation of Stokes theorem due to Élie Cartan:

Theorem 2.1 *Stokes-Cartan Theorem: Suppose M is a compact oriented k-dimensional manifold with boundary ∂M and α is a smooth $(k-1)$-form on M. Then:*

$$\int_M d\alpha = \int_{\partial M} \alpha \qquad (2.17)$$

As well as generalised Stokes's original theorem in vector calculus, the Stokes-Cartan Theorem also embodies the fundamental theorem of calculus and the Gauss divergence theorem. We can see the first relation rather trivially by considering the integration of the differential of a function, df, along a curve in $\mathbb{R}^3$ with endpoints a and b. That is, applying Theorem 2.1 in the case of a 0-form integrated over a 1-dimensional manifold with 0-dimensional boundaries $\{a, b\}$:

$$\int_{[a,b]} df = \int_{\partial[a,b]} f = f(b) - f(a) \qquad (2.18)$$

BOX 2 THE EXTERIOR AND INTERIOR DERIVATIVE

Let M be a manifold. Then there is a unique family of mappings $d^k(U)$: $\Omega^k(U) \to \Omega^{k+1}(U), k = 0 \ldots n$, and U is open in M, such that the exterior derivative, denoted d, has the properties of being a closed, local, anti-derivation of the exterior algebra that reduces to the differential for $k = 0$. The property of being an anti-derivation in this context means that:

$$d(\alpha \wedge \beta) = d\alpha \wedge \beta + (-1)^k \alpha \wedge d\beta \qquad (2.19)$$

for $\alpha \in \Omega^k(U)$ and $\beta \in \Omega^l(U)$ (Abraham & Marsden, 1980, Theorem 2.4.5). Let M be a manifold, X a tangent vector field, and α a $(k+1)$-form. Then the interior derivative $\iota_X \alpha$ is defined by:

$$\iota_X \alpha(X_1 \ldots X_k) = \alpha(X, X_1 \ldots X_k) \qquad (2.20)$$

where $\iota_X \alpha = 0$ for $k = 0$. The interior product is an anti-derivation of the exterior algebra and can be proved to be such that it maps k-forms to $(k-1)$-forms. That is, we have that $\iota_X : \Omega^k(M) \to \Omega^{k-1}(M), k = 1 \ldots n$. (Abraham & Marsden, 1980, Theorem 2.4.13).

The fourth and final operation on differential forms is the *Lie derivative*, $\mathcal{L}$. The Lie derivative of a differential form with respect to a vector field, $\mathcal{L}_X \alpha$, is a linear, derivation operation on the space of differential forms that commutes with the exterior derivative and is such that it maps k-forms to k-forms. The Lie derivative allows us to analyse how a geometric object on a manifold varies under the flow induced by a vector field on that manifold. In particular, the Lie derivative provides us with a means of comparing vector fields and differential before and after they are acted upon by the flow of a vector field.

Most straightforwardly, we can understand the Lie derivative of a function, f, with respect to the flow induced by a vector field, X, as telling us how f changes under the infinitesimal flow generated by X. In the exponential representation of a flow what we are doing in calculating the Lie derivative is then equivalent to evaluating $f(\exp(\epsilon X)x)$ as ϵ varies. We thus have that:

$$\frac{d}{d\epsilon}f(\exp(\epsilon X)x) = X^i(\exp(\epsilon X)x)\frac{\partial f}{\partial x^i}(\exp(\epsilon X)x) \qquad (2.21)$$

$$= X(f)(\exp(\epsilon X)x) \qquad (2.22)$$

so for $\epsilon = 0$ we have that:

$$\left.\frac{d}{d\epsilon}\right|_{\epsilon=0} f(\exp(\epsilon X)x) = X^i \partial_i f(x) = X(f)(x) \equiv \mathcal{L}_X f(x) \qquad (2.23)$$

The Lie derivative of a function therefore reduces to the ordinary directional derivative in the direction picked out by the vector field. (Olver, 2000, pp. 30-1).

The Lie derivative of a vector field with respect to another vector field is called the Lie bracket of two vector fields. It is the unique vector field $\mathcal{L}_X Y \equiv [X, Y]$ satisfying:

$$[X, Y] = \left(X^j \partial_j Y^i - Y^j \partial_j X^i\right) \partial_i \qquad (2.24)$$

for $X = X^i \partial_i$ and $Y = Y^i \partial_i$. We can conceive the Lie bracket of two vector fields geometrically as the infinitesimal commuter of one-parameter groups associated with the two vector fields, $\exp(\epsilon X)$ and $\exp(\epsilon Y)$.

The Lie bracket defines an algebraic structure called a *Lie algebra*. In particular, if we consider the space of vector fields on a manifold $X, Y \in \mathfrak{X}(M)$ then the Lie bracket $[X, Y]$ on $\mathfrak{X}(M)$ together with the real vector space structure of $\mathfrak{X}(M)$ induces a Lie algebra since satisfies the three conditions:

1. *Bilinear*: $[aX + bY, Z] = a[X, Z] + b[Y, Z]$ for all real scalars a, b
2. *Alternativity*: $[X, X] = 0, \forall X \in \mathfrak{X}(M)$
3. *Jacobi Identity*: $[X, [Y, Z]] + [Y, Z, X]] + [Z, [X, Y]] = 0, \forall X, Y, Z \in \mathfrak{X}(M)$

These conditions imply that the Lie bracket is skew symmetric, so $[X, Y] = -[Y, X]$ and it is possible to define a Lie algebra via bilinearity, skew symmetry and the Jacobi identity. See (Abraham & Marsden, 1980, p.85) and (Holm, 2011, §1.7) for more details.

The Lie derivative of 1-forms can be calculated straightforwardly based upon the fact that the $\mathcal{L}$ and $\boldsymbol{d}$ operations commute. This means that we have that:

$$\mathcal{L}_X \theta = \mathcal{L}_X(f_k dx^k) = f_k(\mathcal{L}_X dx^k) + X(f_k) dx^k = f_k d(X(x^k)) + X(f_k) dx^k \quad (2.25)$$

a short calculation shows that the final expression on the right is equivalent to:

$$\iota_X d(f_k dx^k) + d(\iota_X(f_k dx^k)) = \iota_X d\theta + d(\iota_X \theta) = \mathcal{L}_X \theta \quad (2.26)$$

The final expression is a special case of *Cartan's magic formula* which gives us a general equivalence between Lie derivatives and the combination of interior and exterior derivatives:

$$\mathcal{L}_X \alpha = \iota_X d\alpha + d(\iota_X \alpha) \quad (2.27)$$

A second important special case of Cartan's magic formula is for closed 2-forms $\omega = d\theta$:

$$\mathcal{L}_X \omega = \mathcal{L}_X d\theta = \iota_X d(d\theta) + d(\iota_X d\theta) = d(\iota_X d\theta) = d(\iota_X \omega) \quad (2.28)$$

since $d^2 = 0$. Thus the Lie derivative of a closed 2-form with respect to a vector field X, is equivalent to the exterior derivative of the contraction of that vector field with that 2-form.

The Lie derivative is uniquely suited to expression of the invariance properties of a differential forms since we have that a differential k-form α on a manifold M is invariant under the flow of a vector field X if and only if $\mathcal{L}_X \alpha = 0$. (Olver, 2000, Proposition 1.65). A similar result holds for vector fields. Intuitively the idea is that since the Lie derivative gives us an expression for the behaviour of a geometric object (form, vector field, or more general tensor field) as it is dragged along the flow generated by a vector field. The vanishing of the Lie derivative is necessary and sufficient for invariance under the relevant flow.

It will be useful to be able to talk precisely about how maps on manifolds transfer onto the differential objects defined on them.[1] A *diffeomophisms* is an invertible C^∞-mappings between the manifolds: $\varphi : M \to N$. The transfer of a diffeomorphism onto vector fields of the same rank defined on M and N is then the *push-forward* of the diffeomorphism which we write φ_*. The transfer of a diffeomorphism onto a differential form of the same rank defined on M and N is then the *pull-back* of the diffeomorphism which we write φ^*.

We can then specify the transfer of a diffeomorphism onto the exterior derivative as

$$\varphi^*(d\alpha) = d(\varphi^* \alpha) \quad (2.29)$$

---

[1] See (Malament, 2012, §1.5) for more details.

and onto the interior derivative as:

$$\varphi^*(\iota_X \alpha) = \iota_{(\varphi_* X)}(\varphi^* \alpha) \qquad (2.30)$$

The first expression simply amounts to saying that the exterior derivative operation commutes with the pull-back of a diffeomorphism. The second, implies that we can construct the pull-back of a diffeomorphism onto the interior derivative by applying the push-forward operation to the vector field and the pull-back operation to the differential form.

If we combine these expressions with Cartan's magic formulae then we can write the pull-back of the Lie derivative of a differential form with respect to a vector field simply as:

$$\varphi^*(\mathcal{L}_X \alpha) = \varphi^*(\iota_X d\alpha + d(\iota_X \alpha)) \qquad (2.31)$$
$$= \iota_{(\varphi_* X)} d(\varphi^* \alpha) + d(\iota_{(\varphi_* X)} \varphi^* \alpha) \qquad (2.32)$$

These relations will prove of particular value later.

Box 3 The Lie Derivative

Define the pull-back of the flow of a vector field X as:

$$\phi_\epsilon^* \equiv \exp(\epsilon X)^* = \wedge_k T^* M|_{\exp(\epsilon X)x} \to \wedge_k T^* M|_x . \qquad (2.33)$$

Let X be a vector field on M and α be a differential k-form defined on M. The Lie derivative of α with respect to X is the k-form whose value at $x \in M$ is given by:

$$\mathcal{L}_X \alpha|_x \equiv \lim_{\epsilon \to 0} \frac{\phi^*(\alpha|_{\exp(\epsilon X)x}) - \alpha|_x}{\epsilon} = \frac{d}{d\epsilon}\bigg|_{\epsilon=0} \phi^*(\alpha|_{\exp(\epsilon X)x}) \qquad (2.34)$$

(Olver, 2000, Definition 1.63).

This concludes our brief review of differential forms and the four basic operations of wedge product, interior product, exterior derivative, and lie derivative. In the next section we will see how the language of differential forms allows for a natural geometric rendering of Hamiltonian mechanics defined by a special type of 2-form called the *symplectic 2-form*.

3 Symplectic Geometry and Phase Space Mechanics

> ... la physique est de la géométrie — *géométrie symplectique*.
>
> (Gotay & Isenberg, 1992, p. 238)

3.1 Symplectic Geometry and Hamiltonian Systems

In this section we will analyse the geometric structure of Hamiltonian mechanics understood as *symplectic structure*. In particular, we will show how Hamilton's equations can be written in the language of differential forms with the operations on differential forms defined in the previous section applied to the *symplectic* 2-form that is intrinsic to the geometric structure of phase spaces.

The world 'symplectic' was coined by Herman Weyl and means interwoven or plaited. As we shall see, the term is an apposite one since it is precisely the symplectic structure that encodes the interweaving of the canonical position and momentum coordinates with both each other and the dynamics. Here we will primarily follow Abraham and Marsden (1980).

We start by introducing the idea of a *non-degenerate* differential 2-form. Consider a 2-form acting on a pair of vector fields $\omega(X, Y)$. We say that ω is non-degenerate when we have that $\omega(X, Y) = 0, \forall X$ implies that $Y = 0$. Conversely, a degenerate 2-form is such that there is a $Y \neq 0$ such that $\omega(X, Y) = 0, \forall X$. This is equivalent to a non-degenerate 2-form having a trivial *kernel*, or nullspace, and a degenerate 2-form having a non-trivial kernel. These definitions generalise to k-forms. However, the 2-form case is all we will need for the definition of symplectic structure.

It can be proven that a 2-form on a manifold M is non-degenerate if and only if M has an even dimension, $2n$, and $\omega^n = \omega \wedge \ldots \wedge \omega$ is a volume form on M that we write as:

$$\Omega_\omega = \frac{(-1)^{[n/2]}}{n!} \omega^n \tag{3.1}$$

A manifold admits a nowhere-vanishing volume form if and only if it is orientable and thus we have that the existence of a non-degenerate two form on a manifold is necessary and sufficient for the manifold to be orientable. See (Abraham & Marsden, 1980, §3.1) for more details.

We are now able to state the pivotal theorem of Darboux which, in this context, means that given a closed, non-degenerate 2-form on a manifold, there is a local coordinate system at every point in which the form has a canonical coordinate expression. The theorem can be stated as follows:

Theorem 3.1 *Darboux's theorem: Suppose ω is a non-degenerate 2-form on a 2n-dimensional M. Then $d\omega = 0$ if and only if there is a chart (U, φ) at each $m \in M$ such that $\varphi(m) = 0$ and with $\varphi(u) = (x^1(u) \ldots x^n(u), y^1(u) \ldots y^n(u))$ we have that:*

$$\omega|_U = \sum_{i=1}^{n} dx^i \wedge dy^i \tag{3.2}$$

(Abraham & Marsden, 1980, Theorem 3.2.2)

Let us then define a *symplectic form* as a closed, non-degenerate 2-form, ω, on a manifold, M. A *symplectic manifold*, (M, ω), is then given by a pairing of a manifold, M, together with a symplectic form on M. Application of Darboux's theorem to symplectic manifolds establishes the existence of a special set of symplectic charts where the component functions x^i, y^i are *canonical coordinates*, which we will write as q^i, p^i to foreshadow the application to Hamiltonian systems. We are thus guaranteed to be able to locally express the symplectic form as:

$$\omega = \sum_{i=1}^{n} dq^i \wedge dp^i \tag{3.3}$$

and volume form as:

$$\Omega_\omega = dq^1 \wedge \ldots \wedge dq^n \wedge dp^1 \wedge \ldots \wedge dp^n. \tag{3.4}$$

By the Riesz representation theorem (Abraham & Marsden, 1980, Theorem 2.6.9). we are guaranteed that for any orientable manifold, M, with volume form Ω, there is a unique measure μ_Ω such that for every continuous function of compact support we have that:

$$\int f d\mu_\Omega = \int f \Omega \tag{3.5}$$

See (Souriau, 2012, §16) for a detailed introduction to the definitions of measures on manifolds. N.B. strictly the measure μ_Ω should be defined on the *Borel sets U of M*. We will provide an explicit definition of the Borel sets of $\mathbb{R}^N$ in the context of probability measures in Section 4.1.

For a symplectic manifold the unique measure associated to the volume form, Ω_ω, is the Liouville measure μ_{Ω_ω}. In coordinates, the Liouville measure can be expressed as:

$$\mu_{\Omega_\omega} = \int_U \Omega_\omega = \int_U dq^1 \wedge \ldots \wedge dq^n \wedge dp^1 \wedge \ldots \wedge dp^n. \tag{3.6}$$

For most physical purposes we are interested in symplectic manifolds that are phase spaces. That is, symplectic manifolds that are the cotangent bundles, T^*Q, to a configuration space, Q. Cotangent bundles of manifolds are always symplectic manifolds. This is because a canonical 1-form or *symplectic potential*, θ, is defined on the cotangent bundle to any manifold and we can we can always define a symplectic two form, ω, in terms of the exterior derivative of the symplectic potential, $\omega = d\theta$ (Abraham & Marsden, 1980, Theorem 3.2.10).

In finite dimensions with $(q^1 \ldots q^n)$ coordinates on Q and $(q^1 \ldots q^n, p_1 \ldots p_n)$ coordinates on T^*Q we can provide local expressions for symplectic potential of the form:

$$\theta = p_i dq^i \tag{3.7}$$

which means the symplectic 2-form is given by:

$$\omega = d\theta = dp^i \wedge dq_i \tag{3.8}$$

The matrix representation of symplectic 2-form ω is given by:

$$J = \begin{pmatrix} 0 & I \\ -I & 0 \end{pmatrix} \tag{3.9}$$

where I is the identity. The matrix is easily seen to be skew-symmetric and non-singular.

We can now define a Hamiltonian system as follows. Let (M, ω) by a symplectic manifold and $H : M \rightarrow \mathbb{R}$ a C^r function. Define the Hamiltonian vector field, X_H by the condition:

$$\iota_{X_H} \omega = dH \tag{3.10}$$

then (M, ω, X_H) is a *Hamiltonian system* and H is the *Hamiltonian function*. Given an arbitrary vector field Y we can write this equation equivalently as:

$$\omega(X_H, Y) = dH(Y) \tag{3.11}$$

The non-degeneracy of ω guarantees that X_H exists. On connected symplectic manifolds any two Hamiltonians for the same Hamiltonian vector field differ by a constant.

Now, let $(q^1 \ldots q^n, p_1 \ldots p_n)$ be coordinates for ω so that we have that $\omega = dp^i \wedge dq_i$ then the Hamiltonian vector field takes the form:

$$X_H = \left(\frac{\partial H}{\partial p_i}, -\frac{\partial H}{\partial q^i} \right) \tag{3.12}$$

The integral curves of X_H are the $\gamma(t) = (q(t), p(t))$ for which Hamilton's equations hold:

$$\dot{q} = \frac{\partial H}{\partial p_i}, \quad \dot{p} = \frac{\partial H}{\partial q^i} \tag{3.13}$$

for $i = 1 \ldots n$. Thus we can understand (3.10) *as* Hamilton's equations.

The skew symmetry of ω together with (3.11) then directly implies conservation of the Hamiltonian function, typically interpreted as an energy function, since for any Hamiltonian system (M, ω, X_H) we have that the evaluation of the Hamiltonian function on the integral curves $H(\gamma(t))$ will be constant in t:

$$\frac{d}{dt} H(\gamma(t)) = \omega(X_H(\gamma(t)), X_H(\gamma(t))) = 0 \tag{3.14}$$

(Abraham & Marsden, 1980, Proposition 3.3.3)

We thus see that the basic dynamical features of Hamiltonian mechanics are encoded in the symplectic structure of phase space. In particular, symplectic structure is in an important sense intrinsic to phase spaces and given such structure and an energy function we are guaranteed to be able to define a Hamiltonian system that in turn provides a unique (up to a constant) representation of energy-conserving dynamics. In the following section we will consider a mild generalisation of the conversation property of the dynamics in terms of the conversation of phase-space volume in a Hamiltonian system, as implied via a geometric version of Liouville's Theorem.

3.2 Liouville's Theorem and the Poisson Bracket

The defining feature of the geometrisation of mechanics as we have explored it thus far is the consideration of properties of *families of solutions* in a state space. It is the structure of such families that the symplectic structure of phase space pertains. This feature will prove crucial to our more interpretative discussion of geometric representations of mechanical systems in Section 8. In the present section we will focus our attention a key formal property of families of solutions in phase space: the conversation of phase space volume.

A simple intuitive picture of the content of Liouville's Theorem can be provided by considering the instantaneous state of a finite ensemble of identical mechanical systems with differing initial conditions, corresponding to a finite region of phase space. Consider the flow of the Hamiltonian vector field at every point in our region and imagine following this flow for a finite time. In such a way we can define a second region of phase space corresponding to the time evolution of our ensemble. The theorem states that the two regions occupy the same volume. In formal terms, following (Abraham & Marsden, 1980, Proposition 3.3.4), we can state the result as follows:

Theorem 3.2 *Liouville's Theorem : Let (M, ω, X_H) be a Hamiltonian system and $\phi(t)$ be the flow of the Hamiltonian vector field X_H. Then for each t we have that $\phi_*(t)\omega = \omega$ and thus that $\phi(t)$ also preserves the volume form Ω_ω.*

A geometric basis for the theorem is straightforward to establish if we recall that Cartan's magic formula for closed 2-forms $\omega = d\theta$ given in (2.28) was:

$$\mathcal{L}_X \omega = d(\iota_X \omega).$$

The geometric form of Liouville's Theorem then immediately follows from the definition of the Hamiltonian vector field, the Lie derivative, and the exterior product, since we have that:

$$\frac{d}{dt}\phi_*(t)\omega = \phi_*(t)\mathcal{L}_{X_H}\omega$$
$$= \phi_*(t)(d(\iota_{X_H}\omega)) = \phi_*(t)(d(dH))$$
$$= 0$$

which implies that $\phi_*(t)\omega = \omega$ which, in turn, implies that $\phi(t)$ preserves the volume form Ω_ω. We have thus distilled the geometric essence of Liouville's theorem to the simple statement that:

$$\mathcal{L}_{X_H}\omega = 0 \tag{3.15}$$

which is true for any Hamiltonian system (M, ω, X_H).

A further important result, which is also often called Liouville's Theorem, is that the unique Liouville measure μ_{Ω_ω}, associated to the volume form, Ω_ω, is also conserved under the infinitesimal transformation associated with any Hamiltonian vector field defined on a symplectic manifold. This means that the Liouville measure is conserved by the dynamics and, more generally, under any symplectomorphism (Souriau, 2012, Theorem 16.99).[2]

We will return to this important result in the context of our discussion of probability and phase space statistical mechanics in Section 4.3.

Let (M, ω) be a symplectic manifold and f and g be functions on M. We can then define the *Poisson bracket* of f and g via the action of the ω on the induced vector fields X_f and X_g:

$$\{f,g\} = \omega(X_f, X_g) \tag{3.16}$$

Which can be expressed in terms of the Lie derivative as:

$$\{f,g\} = -\mathcal{L}_{X_f}g = \mathcal{L}_{X_g}f \tag{3.17}$$

The Poisson bracket of two functions thus corresponds to the Lie bracket of the associated vector fields.

The space of real valued smooth functions over a symplectic manifold forms a particular type of Lie algebra called a *Poisson algebra* where the Lie bracket satisfies the usual conditions given earlier together with the further condition of obeying *Leibniz's rule*: $\{fg, h\} = f\{g, h\} + g\{f, h\}$. Manifolds equipped with such a bracket operation are called *Poisson manifolds* and all symplectic manifolds can be shown to be Poisson manifolds (the converse does not hold). For more details see (Marsden, 1992, §2).

---

[2] This result is an exemplification of the much more general property that any measure defined via the integral of a volume form will be invariant under *orientation persevering* diffeomorphisms (Lee, 2003, Prop. 16.6).

Using the relation between the Lie derivative and Poisson bracket, it is not difficult to show that in canonical coordinates $(q^1 \ldots q^n, p_1 \ldots p_n)$ the Poisson bracket takes the familiar form:

$$\{f,g\} = \frac{\partial f}{\partial q^i}\frac{\partial g}{\partial p_i} - \frac{\partial f}{\partial p_i}\frac{\partial g}{\partial q^i} \tag{3.18}$$

(Abraham & Marsden, 1980, Corollary 3.3.14)

Let us then consider the Hamilton vector, X_H field on a symplectic manifold, and associated flow $\phi(t)$. For any function on the manifold, f, we have that:

$$\frac{d}{dt}\phi_*(t)f = \phi_*(t)\mathcal{L}_{X_H}f = \{\phi_*(t)f, H\} \tag{3.19}$$

A more concise and familiar expression is to write (3.19) simply as:

$$\dot{f} = \{f, H\} \tag{3.20}$$

which is the equation of motion in Poisson bracket form (Marsden & Ratiu, 2013). We can then express energy conversation in the form $\{H, H\} = 0$ and express that a function g on M is a constant of motion relative to X_H by writing simply $\{g, H\} = 0$.

A simple way to approach the more general question of invariants functions is to consider a vector field X_g that is such that $\mathcal{L}_{X_g}\omega = 0$ and $\mathcal{L}_{X_g}H = 0$. That is, a symplectomorphism that preserves the Hamiltonian. Such transformations will preserve the integral curves of X_H and thus the infinitesimal transformations generated by X_g are *symmetry transformations* in the generalised sense that they map dynamically possible models into dynamically possible models (Gryb & Thébault, 2023).

In such circumstances, we will have that $\{g, H\} = 0$ where g is the Hamiltonian function defined by relation $dg = \iota_{X_g}d\omega$. This means that every symmetry transformations generated by the flow of some vector field X_g that preserves ω has an associated conserved charge g. This result has been called the *symplectic Noether theorem* and expresses the deep interweaving between symmetry, conversation, and the symplectic structure of Hamiltonian systems.

3.3 Symplectomorphisms

The final feature of symplectic mechanics that we shall consider is the perhaps the most subtle and certainly the most beautiful. In simple terms, the feature in question is that the canonical coordinate charts that we lay upon a symplectic manifold do not have physical significance. Rather, the *structure* of a mechanical theory within the symplectic representation is encoded in the Hamilton vector field which is independent of the canonical coordinate chart.

We can capture the content of this idea more precisely by considering the general form of transformations between manifolds defined by diffeomorphisms. Recall that diffeomorphisms are invertible C^∞-mappings between the manifolds: $\varphi : M \to N$. Let us consider a pair of symplectic $2n$-dimensional manifolds, (M, ω) and (N, ρ). If the push-forward of the diffeomorphism φ preserves the symplectic structure, that is, we have that $\varphi_* \rho = \omega$, then we say that φ is a *symplectomorphism* or canonical transformation.

The most crucial feature of symplectomorphisms is their action on the Hamilton vector field defined via (3.10). The general form of this action can be proved via a theorem attributed to Jacobi (Abraham & Marsden, 1980, Theorem 3.3.9) and can be concisely stated as:

$$\varphi_* X_H = X_{H \circ \varphi} \qquad (3.21)$$

Since, as noted earlier, on connected symplectic manifolds any two Hamiltonians for the same Hamiltonian vector field differ by a constant, we then have that the symplectomorphisms leave the dynamical structure encoded in the Hamiltonian vector field unchanged. The proof of (3.21) is straightforward and instructive so we will provide a brief reconstruction here.

First, re-write Hamilton's equations (3.10) for the Hamiltonian function given by the composition $H \circ \varphi$:

$$\iota_{X_{H \circ \varphi}} \omega = d(H \circ \varphi) \qquad (3.22)$$

Second, apply the push-forward of the symplectomorphism to the original form of Hamilton's equations (3.10) using our transfer equations (2.29) and (2.30):

$$\iota_{(\varphi_* X_H)}(\varphi_* \omega) = \varphi_* dH \qquad (3.23)$$
$$= d(H \circ \varphi) \qquad (3.24)$$

Then equating our two expressions gives:

$$\iota_{X_{H \circ \varphi}} \omega = \iota_{(\varphi_* X_H)}(\varphi_* \omega) \qquad (3.25)$$

We then have by definition that $\varphi_* \omega = \omega$ and so application of Hamilton's equations once more finally gives us:

$$X_{H \circ \varphi} = \varphi_* X_H. \qquad (3.26)$$

Symplectomorphisms both preserve the volume form and allow us to transform between the local symplectic charts defined on the two manifolds. They are also the crucial ingredient in the theory of canonical transformations and the Hamilton-Jacobi formulation of mechanics.

Abstractly speaking, *symplectomorphisms are the isomorphism of the category of symplectic manifolds*. On that basis we might plausibly interpret a given symplectic manifold, (M,ω), to be defined only up to symplectomorphism. We will consider this feature in our more interpretative discussion of geometric representations of mechanical systems in Section 8.

3.4 Classical Harmonic Oscillator

Consider a Newtonian system with one spatial degrees of freedom q and potential $V(q) = \frac{1}{2}kq^2$ in some preferred chat. The phase space is a two dimensional symplectic manifold. The Hamiltonian of the system is:

$$H = \frac{p^2}{2m} + \frac{1}{2}kq^2 \qquad (3.27)$$

and the associated Hamiltonian vector field:

$$X_H = \left(\frac{p}{m}, -kq\right) \qquad (3.28)$$

The geometric form of this vector field is illustrated in Figure 2.

The integral curves of X_H are the $\gamma(t) = (q(t), p(t))$ for which Hamilton's equations hold:

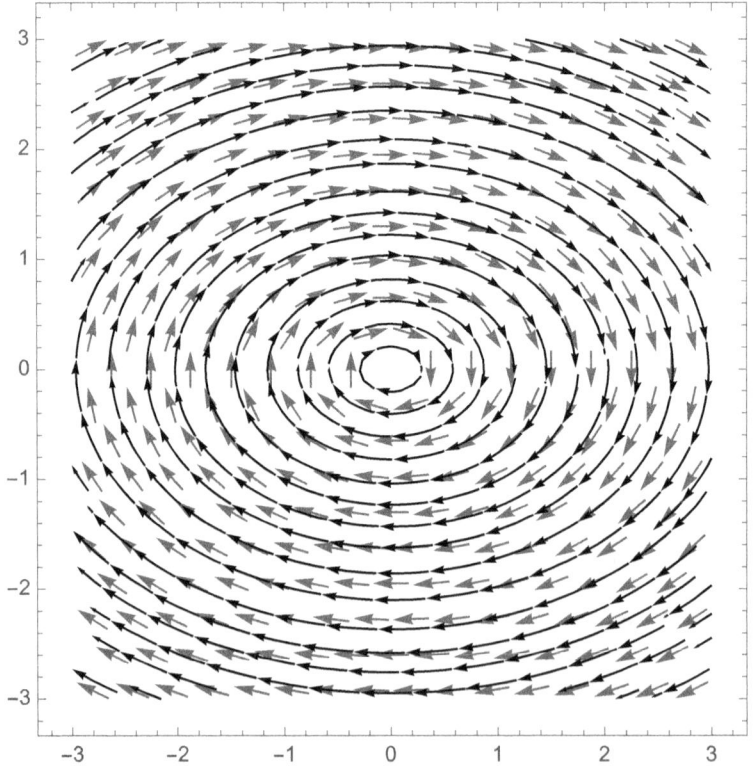

Figure 2 Phase portrait showing the Hamiltonian vector field and corresponding integral curves of a simple harmonic oscillator for a specific set of parameter values. Generated with *Mathematica*

$$\dot{q} = \frac{p}{m}, \dot{p} = -kq \quad (3.29)$$

which are obviously equivalent to Newton's second law since the two equations imply that:

$$\ddot{q} = -\frac{k}{m}q \quad (3.30)$$

which means we have the familiar solutions of $q(t) = A\cos(\omega t) + B\sin(\omega t)$ for $\omega = \sqrt{k/m}$.

If the initial position and momentum are q_0 and p_0 then we will have that $A = q_0$ and $B = \frac{p_0}{\sqrt{mk}}$ and thus that the general solutions are given by:

$$q(t) = q_0 \cos(\omega t) + \frac{p_0}{\sqrt{mk}} \sin(\omega t) \quad (3.31)$$

$$p(t) = -m\omega q_0 \sin(\omega t) + p_0 \cos(\omega t) \quad (3.32)$$

Liouville's theorem then implies conservation of phase space area along the Hamiltonian flow in question. Geometrically this can be visualised as the constant area of a rotating quadrilateral picked out by a bundle of contiguous trajectories.

3.5 Further Topics of Study

- The Symplectic Noether theorem (Souriau, 1974, p. 357), (Kostant, 1970) (Kosmann-Schwarzbach, 2010, p108).
- Symplectic Reduction and Philosophy of Symmetry (Belot, 2007; Bradley, 2024a; Butterfield, 2007; Rickles, 2007; Thébault, 2011).
- Symplectic Structure and Theoretical Equivalence (Barrett, 2019; Bradley, 2024b; Curiel, 2014; Dewar, 2022; North, 2009)
- Anti-Symplectomorphisms and Time-Reversal Symmetry (Roberts, 2022).

4 Probability and Statistical Phase Space Mechanics

> If we regard a phase as represented by a point in space of $2n$ dimensions, the changes which take place in the course of time in our ensemble of systems will be represented by a current in such space. This current will be steady so long as the external coordinates are not varied. In any case the current will satisfy a law which in its various expressions is analogous to the hydrodynamic law which may be expressed by the phrases *conservation of volumes or conservation of density about a moving point*.

(Gibbs, 1902, p.11)

4.1 Measures and Probability Densities Functions

In this section we provide a brief introduction to some of the core mathematical concepts for the representation of phase space probability measures in statistical mechanics. We will assume basic concepts from elementary set theory. Our aim is to introduce the core formal notions of a σ-*algebra*, a *probability measure*, the *Borel sets* of $\mathbb{R}$, *Lebesgue integrability*, and a *probability density function*. We will principally follow (Dudley, 2010, §-3-4) and (Breuer & Petruccione, 2002, §1). See also (Feller, 1991, §IV) for further technical details. Additional sources will be noted where relevant.

Consider a set, Ω, which is non-empty. Let us designate this set the *sample space*. Now consider a non-empty collection of subsets, $\mathfrak{A}$, that we designate the *event algebra*. The event algebra is then a σ-*algebra* iff the following three conditions hold:

1. The sample space and the empty set belong to the event algebra, that is, $\emptyset \in \mathfrak{A}, \Omega \in \mathfrak{A}$.
2. The elements of the event algebra are closed under complementation, that is, $\Omega \setminus \sigma \in \mathfrak{A}$ for all $\sigma \in \mathfrak{A}$.
3. The elements of the event algebra are closed under countable union, that is, $A_1 \cup A_2 \cup A_3, \ldots, \in \mathfrak{A}$ for all $A_1, A_2, \sigma_3, \ldots, \in \mathfrak{A}$.

The third condition is crucial for the algebra to be a σ-algebra. One can define an algebra of events that is not a σ-algebra by weakening the condition, for example to finite union.

BOX 4 ADDITIVITY AND MEASURE SPACES

Following (Dudley, 2010, pp.85–87), let X be a set and $\mathcal{C}$ be a collection of subsets of X with $\emptyset \in \mathcal{C}$. Consider a *set function* μ which is a function from $\mathcal{C}$ into the extended real line $[-\infty, \infty] \equiv \{-\infty\} \cup \mathbb{R} \cup \{\infty\}$.

We say that the set function μ is *finitely additive* iff $\mu(\emptyset) = 0$ and whenever $A_i \in \mathcal{C}$ for $i = 1, \ldots, n$ are disjoint and

$$A \equiv \bigcup_{i=1}^{n} A_i \in \mathcal{C} \tag{4.1}$$

we have that

$$\mu(A) = \sum_{i=1}^{n} \mu(A_i) \tag{4.2}$$

If, additionally, we have that whenever $A_n \in \mathcal{C}, n = 1, 2, \ldots, A_n$ are disjoint and $B \equiv \cup_{n \geq 1} A_n \in \mathcal{C}$, we have that

$$\mu(B) = \sum_{n \geq 1} \mu(A_n) \tag{4.3}$$

then μ is *countably additive*.

For any set X the power set 2^X is the collection of all subsets of X. A collection of subsets $\mathfrak{A} \subset 2^X$ is a *ring* iff $\emptyset \in \mathcal{A}$ and for all A and B in $\mathcal{A}$ we have that $A \cup B \in \mathcal{A}$ and $B \setminus A \in \mathcal{A}$. A ring is an *algebra* iff $X \in \mathfrak{A}$. We then have that an algebra is a σ-*algebra* if for any sequence $\{A_n\}$ of sets in $\mathfrak{A}$, $\cup_{n \geq 1} A_n \in \mathfrak{A}$. A countably additive function μ from a σ-algebra S of subsets of X into $[0, \infty]$ is then a *measure* and a triple $[X, S, \mu]$ is a *measure space*.

A *probability measure* is a set function $p : \mathcal{A} \to \mathbb{R}$ which assigns a real number $p(A)$ to every event A in a σ-algebra, that is, we have that $A \mapsto p(A) \in \mathbb{R}$, such that the following three conditions hold:

1. The probability of any event lies in the unit interval, that is, for all $A \in \mathcal{A}$ we have that $0 \leq p(A) \leq 1$.
2. The total probability is normalised to one across the sample space, that is, $p(\Omega) = 1$.
3. If we have a countable collection of disjoint events the probability of their union is equal to the sum of their probabilities, that is, we have that if

   $A_1, \ldots, A_n, \ldots \in \mathcal{A}$ with $A_i \cap A_j = \emptyset$ for $i \neq j$

   then

   $$p(\cup_{n=1}^{\infty} A_n) = \sum_{n=1}^{\infty} \mu(A_n) \tag{4.4}$$

The last condition of σ-additivity is crucial for the measure to be a probability measure. It can be weakened to define a set function that is not a probability measure for example since it is only a finitely additive quasi-measure. We will consider the case of quasi-measures when we examine the quantum phase space formalism in Section 6.

In general terms, we can think of any specification of a triple of sample space, σ-algebra and probability measure as a *probability model*, $(\Omega, \mathfrak{A}, p)$. Realisations of such a model can then be provided by specifying representations of the relevant σ-algebra and probability measure in terms of specific sets of objects with the appropriate algebraic structure and functions with the appropriate properties.

The most important σ-algebra found in the formalisation of physical theory is that generated by the topology of $\mathbb{R}$. In particular, we can understand the *Borel sets* of $\mathbb{R}$ as being given by the smallest σ-algebra which contains all the open and closed intervals of the real line.[3] We will denote the Borel sets of the real line as $\mathcal{B}(\mathbb{R})$.

There is guaranteed to exists a measure on $\mathcal{B}(\mathbb{R})$ defined on the closed interval $(a, b]$ of the real numbers in terms of the distance measure $\mu_L((a, b]) = b - a$ for any real $a \leq b$ (Dudley, 2010, Theorem 3.2.6). The measure μ_L is called the *Lebesgue measure* on $\mathbb{R}$ and can be naturally extended to a real space of arbitrary finite dimension $\mathbb{R}^N$ in terms of a volume measure μ_L^N which allows us to pick out the class of Lebesgue measurable subsets of $\mathbb{R}^N$. The Borel sets of $\mathcal{B}(\mathbb{R}^N)$ are the most physically important example of Lebesgue measurable sets. A function $f: \mathbb{R}^N \to \mathbb{R}$ is then *Lebesgue measurable* if the pre-image of every Borel set under the function is a Lebesgue measurable set.

The final element in the formalisation of probability theory for a state space application is the idea of a density function. This in turn requires us to define what it is for a function to be integrable on $\mathbb{R}^N$. Eliding some considerable formal subtleties (Dudley, 2010, §4) we can do this rather directly in terms of the Lebesgue measure by specifying that a Lebesgue measurable function $f: \mathbb{R}^N \to \mathbb{R}$ is *Lebesgue integrable* iff we have that:

$$\int_{\mathbb{R}^N} |f(x)| \, d\mu_L^N(x) < \infty \tag{4.5}$$

We can then introduce a *probability density function* as a function $f: \mathbb{R}^N \to \mathbb{R}$ that is Lebesgue integrable and defines a probability measure $p(B)$ over the Borel sets of $\mathbb{R}^N$ given by the formula:

$$p(B) = \int_B f(x) d\mu_L^N(x) \tag{4.6}$$

where $B \in \mathcal{B}$.

Since have demanded that $p(B)$ defines a probability measure, we will automatically have that three conditions aforementioned hold. We can restate these conditions explicitly as follows:

1. The probability density associated with any sub-region of $\mathbb{R}^N$ lies in the unit interval, that is, for all $B \in \mathcal{B}$ we have that $0 \leq p(B) \leq 1$.
2. The probability density is normalised to one across $\mathbb{R}^N$, that is, we have that

---

[3] See (Dudley, 2010, p.98) for a more full definition.

$$p(\Omega) = \int_{\mathbb{R}^N} f(x) d\mu_L^N(x) = 1 \qquad (4.7)$$

3. If we have a countable collection of disjoint regions of $\mathbb{R}^N$, the probability of their union is equal to the sum of their probabilities, that is, we have that if

$$B_1, \ldots, B_n, \ldots \in \mathcal{B} \text{ with } B_i \cap B_j = \emptyset \text{ for } i \neq j$$

then

$$p(\cup_{n=1}^{\infty} B_n) = \sum_{n=1}^{\infty} \int_{B_n} f(x) d\mu_L^N(x) \qquad (4.8)$$

The final condition implies that any function which is measurable on the Borel algebra can play the role of a probability density function (PDF) so long as it is positive and norm one across the entire space. Moreover, we also have that a PDF will be Lebesgue measurable by definition. The leads us to the final crucial concept the idea of the *essential support* of a PDF.

The essential support of a function, $\mathrm{ess\ sup}(f)$, indicates the smallest closed subset in the domain of a measurable function such that the function can be zero 'almost' everywhere outside that subset. The 'almost' in this context is cashed out via the measure such that the points which are outside the essential support and where the function is non-zero are of measure zero. For any Lebesgue measurable function f we have that $\mathrm{ess\ sup}(f) = \sup(f)$ (Lieb & Loss, 2001, p.13). The essential support and support of the PDF $f(x)$ is thus given by the smallest possible region in $\mathbb{R}^N$ such that the function can be zero (almost) everywhere else. These are the singleton elements of the Borel sets points which correspond to the point set $\{x\}$.

We thus have the possibility of picking out an event in the σ-algebra via a point set $\{x\} \in \mathbb{R}^N$ and it is admissible to choose a probability density function which assigns a non-zero value only to a measure zero subset of all other points. This means that it is possible to consider probability density functions that are (almost) entirely concentrated at a single point which amounts to allowing the possibility that the probability density function approximates a δ-function. Correspondingly, since its integral over $\mathbb{R}^N$ is normalised, by concentrating a probability density function almost entirely at one point we must allow that the function is unbounded from above.

These properties will be important for physical interpretation of the deterministic limit of stochastic phase space models considered in Section 4.2. They will also prove relevant in the context quantum phase space representations, in which the point set is not part of the essential support, as discussed in Section 6.1.

4.2 Stochastic Phase Space Models

We will now proceed to combine the formal ingredients developed in the previous section with the phase space representation of mechanics presented in Section 3.1. This will lead us to a stochastic representation of phase space mechanics within which we combine a Hamiltonian mechanical system with a probability density function.

The core elements of a stochastic phase space model are built from the natural structures on Γ. In particular, whereas the symplectic structure induces a Poisson algebraic structure, the topological structure induces a σ-algebraic structure. The crucial link between the two is in terms of the volume measure $dq \wedge dp$ which is *both* the unique Liouville volume form preserved by the Hamiltonian flow as per the discussion of Section 3.2 *and* the natural Lebesgue volume measure on Γ as per the discussion of Section 4.1.

Following, Dawid and Thébault (2025), let us then define a *stochastic phase space model* as a triple $(\Gamma, \mathfrak{O}, \rho)$ with the following properties:

1. **State Space**: $\Gamma = (\mathbb{R}^{2N}, \omega)$ represents the space of possible states of system as a $2N$-dimensional symplectic manifold equipped with the closed non-degenerate two form $\omega = dq \wedge dp$ and associated volume measure $dqdp$ in the Darboux chart;
2. **Observable Algebra**: $\mathfrak{O}$ represents observables as a Poisson algebra given by the space of real-valued smooth functions over Γ with the Cartesian product and Poisson bracket $\{,\}$, the relevant bilinear products. The distinguished function $H \in \mathfrak{O}$ induces a time evolution automorphism via the Poisson bracket: $\frac{d}{dt}A = \{A, H\}$ for all $A \in \mathfrak{O}$.
3. **Probability Density Function**: ρ is a phase space probability density function, $\rho(q,p) : \Gamma \to \mathbb{R}$, which is Lebesgue integrable with respect to the volume measure, $dqdp$, and induces a probability measure, μ, such that for any event with probability, $\mu(B)$, there is a corresponding PDF, $\rho(q,p)$, that satisfies the conditions:
   (a) $\mu(B) \geq 0$ for all $B \in \mathcal{B}$ (positive)
   (b) $\int_\Gamma \rho(q,p) dqdp = 1$ (normalised)
   (c) If $B_1, \ldots, B_n, \ldots \in \mathcal{B}$ with $B_i \cap B_j = \emptyset$ for $i \neq j$ then $\mu(\cup_{n=1}^\infty B_n) = \sum_{n=1}^\infty \int_{B_n} \rho(q,p) dqdp$ (σ-additive)
   where $B \in \mathcal{B}$ are the Borel sets $\mathcal{B}(\mathbb{R}^{2N})$.
4. **Expectation Values**: $\langle A \rangle$ is the expectation value (first moment) of an observable defined as:

$$\langle A \rangle \equiv \int_\Gamma A(q,p) \rho(q,p) dqdp \qquad (4.9)$$

for all $A \in \mathfrak{O}$

A stochastic phase space model provides an interpretation (assignment of meaning) to a classical probabilistic structure as follows: The state space Γ is the sample space Ω. The Borel sets given by sub-regions of phase space $\mathcal{B}(\mathbb{R}^{2N})$ are the σ-algebra. The probability measure $p(B)$ is given by the integration of the probability density function $\rho(q,p)$ with respect to the volume measure $dqdp$ over a sub-region $B \subseteq \mathbb{R}^{2N}$. The model includes a deterministic subset since a function that approximates a δ-function is an admissible PDF and thus the case in which the singleton of the Borel sets is measure (almost) one and (almost) all other points are measure zero is an admissible stochastic phase space model as per our discussion of the essential support earlier.

The model also provides a representation of expectation values of observable functions. That is, it allows us to represent not just the stochastic properties associated with the state of the system but also the stochastic properties observables in terms of the their moments. The first moment being the expectation value as per Equation (4.9). The higher order (raw) moments (i.e. variance, skewness, kurtosis) are then given by the standard formula:

$$\langle A^m \rangle = \int_\Gamma A(q,p)^n \rho(q,p) dq dp \qquad (4.10)$$

where m is the order of the moment. Clearly the expectation values are, like the moments in general, also part of the observable algebra. As such, we can use the Hamiltonian function and the Poisson bracket to describe the evolution equations for the moments. We will derive an explicit form of these equations in terms of the stochastic Ehrenfest equations in Section 4.4 based upon the famous continuity equation due to Liouville that will be derived in the following section.

4.3 Probability Currents and the Liouville Equation

In this section we will review the elementary textbook presentation of the stochastic Liouville's equation following Pathria and Beale (2011). We start by showing how the equation can be derived by thinking of the classical probability density in terms of a 'fluid' with an *incompressible flow*, before considering the relation to the symplectic structure via the geometric presentation of Liouville's theorem that was provided in the previous section.

We start by considering an arbitrary volume B of the phase space with a boundary ∂B. If we think of the probability like a fluid, it is natural to understand there to be a *phase space current J^i* which represents net flow *out* of the region, and is associated with the 'fluid' density $\rho(q,p)$ by the formula:

$$J^i = \rho(q,p) v^i \qquad (4.11)$$

where v^i is just the tuple $(\dot{q}, \dot{p})$ and the other dimensions of phase space are suppressed as per our notation earlier. If n^i is the unit vector normal to the boundary ∂B, we then have that by Gauss's theorem we can write:

$$\int_{\partial B} J^i n_i d(\partial B) = \int_B \partial_i J^i dq dp \tag{4.12}$$

$$= \int_B \left(\dot{q} \frac{\partial \rho}{\partial q} + \dot{p} \frac{\partial \rho}{\partial p} \right) dq dp \tag{4.13}$$

$$= \int_B \{\rho, H\} dq dp \tag{4.14}$$

where we have used Hamilton's equations and the definition of the Poisson bracket.

Now, if we assume the probabilistic equivalent of the continuity equation – that is, the fluid has no 'sources' or 'sinks' – then the rate of change of total probability fluid in an arbitrary region will be equal to the negative of the flux out of the region. Thus, we have that:

$$\frac{\partial}{\partial t} \int_B \rho dq dp = - \int_{\partial B} J^i n_i d(\partial B) \tag{4.15}$$

$$= - \int_B \{\rho, H\} dq dp \tag{4.16}$$

and thus that:

$$\int_B \left(\frac{\partial \rho}{\partial t} + \{\rho, H\} \right) dq dp = 0 \tag{4.17}$$

Finally, we then have that

$$\frac{d\rho}{dt} = \frac{\partial \rho}{\partial t} + \{\rho, H\} = 0 \tag{4.18}$$

since we need to be able to drop the integrals for the equation to hold for arbitrary regions.

Equation (4.18) is the Liouville equation and it means that the total derivative of the probability density is always vanishing in a stochastic Hamiltonian system. Equivalently, the Liouville equation implies that the probability 3-current given by the tuple $(\rho, \rho\dot{q}, \rho\dot{p})$ is always conserved. Intuitively, we can think of the stochastic Liouville equation as implying that the *local* density around a *representative point* as viewed by a co-moving observer stays constant in time (Pathria & Beale, 2011, p. 28), cf. (Gibbs, 1902, p.11). This is the characteristic property of a fluid with an *incompressible flow*.

The Liouville equation has an obvious formal connection to the geometric equation we introduced as Liouville's Theorem in Section 3.2. In that context we saw that for any Hamiltonian system (M, ω, X_H) the Lie drag of the symplectic structure under the dynamics vanishes, that is, $\mathcal{L}_{X_H} \omega = 0$. We also noted that

Classical and Quantum Phase Space Mechanics

a further implication of theorem is that the Liouville measure μ_{Ω_ω}, associated to the volume form, Ω_ω will also be invariant under the dynamics.

The full significance of these results should now be clear. In particular, when combined with the Liouville equation (4.18) it is evident that the additivity property of regions of phase space will be preserved *over time* since both the measure and the local density about a representative point are preserved. There are then two (closely related) ways in which this property can *fail* to hold: the measure may fail to be invariant or the probability 3-current may fail to be locally conserved. The dissipative dynamics displayed by contact Hamiltonian systems considered in Section 5 will exemplify the first possibility and the quantum phase space dynamics of quasi-probability representations considered in Section 6 will exemplify the second.

4.4 The Stochastic Ehrenfest Equations

Let us now study the implications of the Liouville equation for the equation of motion for the statistical moments of the observables. We will restrict to the case in which the form of the Hamiltonian is $H = \frac{1}{2m}p^2 + V(q)$. The Liouville equation then is then:

$$\frac{\partial \rho}{\partial t} = -\{\rho, H\} \tag{4.19}$$

$$= -\frac{p}{m}\frac{\partial \rho}{\partial q} + \frac{\partial V(q)}{\partial q}\frac{\partial \rho}{\partial p} \tag{4.20}$$

The first moment equations (4.9) then take the form:

$$\langle q \rangle = \int_\Gamma q\rho\, dq\, dp \tag{4.21}$$

$$\langle p \rangle = \int_\Gamma p\rho\, dq\, dp \tag{4.22}$$

The equation of motion for $\langle q \rangle$ is straightforwardly derived by taking derivatives and using the first of Hamilton's equations together with the vanishing of the total derivative of ρ to get:

$$\frac{d}{dt}\langle q \rangle = \frac{1}{m}\langle p \rangle \tag{4.23}$$

This is, of course, the Newtonian equation for the momentum in terms of the velocity only expressed in terms of the 'centre of mass' of the probability distribution. By the same approach the equation of motion for $\langle p \rangle$ is given by:

$$\frac{d}{dt}\langle p \rangle = -\int_\Gamma \frac{dV(q)}{dq}\rho\, dq\, dp \tag{4.24}$$

which means that we have that:

$$\frac{d}{dt}\langle p \rangle = -\left\langle \frac{dV(q)}{dq} \right\rangle \tag{4.25}$$

The equation (4.25) allows us to treat the centroid of the distribution as a particle obeying Newton's second law *if* it is true that:

$$\left\langle \frac{dV(q)}{dq} \right\rangle = \frac{dV(\langle q \rangle)}{dq} \tag{4.26}$$

We will thus have that under this condition a classical stochastic version of the Ehrenfest equations will hold and we can understand the centroid of the distribution as being governed by the same equations as a Newtonian point particle in that we get equations of the form $P = m\dot{Q}$ and $\dot{P} = -\nabla V(Q)$ for $Q = \langle q \rangle$ and $P = \langle p \rangle$. The 'if' is all important, however. The stochastic version of the Ehrenfest equations hold *only* under the condition (4.26). Indeed, the equations will not hold, *even approximately*, unless the probability distribution is of suitably narrow width (Ballentine, Yang, & Zibin, 1994).

To establish explicit limits on the validly of the stochastic Ehrenfest equations, following the treatment of Ballentine and McRae (1998), we can expand $V(q)$ in a Taylor series in $\delta q = q - \langle q \rangle$:

$$V(q) = V\langle q \rangle + \sum_{l=1}^{\infty} \frac{(\delta q)^l}{l!} \frac{d^l V(\langle q \rangle)}{d\langle q \rangle^l} \tag{4.27}$$

which implies that:

$$\frac{dV(q)}{dq} = \frac{dV(\langle q \rangle)}{d\langle q \rangle} + \sum_{l=1}^{\infty} \frac{(\delta q)^l}{(l-1)!} \frac{d^{l-1} V(\langle q \rangle)}{d\langle q \rangle^{l-1}} \tag{4.28}$$

where we have used the chain rule and the fact that $\frac{d\langle q \rangle}{dq} = 1$. Substituting this expression into (4.25) means that we have that:

$$\frac{d}{dt}\langle p \rangle = -\left\langle \frac{dV(\langle q \rangle)}{d\langle q \rangle} \right\rangle - \left\langle \sum_{l=1}^{\infty} \frac{(\delta q)^l}{(l-1)!} \frac{d^{l-1} V(\langle q \rangle)}{d\langle q \rangle^{l-1}} \right\rangle \tag{4.29}$$

$$= -\frac{dV(\langle q \rangle)}{d\langle q \rangle} + \sum_{l=1}^{\infty} \frac{\langle(\delta q)^l\rangle}{(l-1)!} \frac{d^{l-1} V(\langle q \rangle)}{d\langle q \rangle^{l-1}} \tag{4.30}$$

where we have assumed that:

$$\left\langle \frac{d^l V(\langle q \rangle)}{d\langle q \rangle^l} \right\rangle = \frac{d^l V(\langle q \rangle)}{d\langle q \rangle^l} \tag{4.31}$$

for all l since $\langle q \rangle$ is just a number rather than a random variable.

This analysis indicates that we can understand the moments, $\langle(\delta q)^l\rangle$ for $l \geq 1$, as parametrising the divergence from the stochastic Ehrenfest equations. For distributions symmetric about the mean, the first moment vanishes, thus we will expect the first deviation to typically be controlled by the size of second moment which is simply the variance. Thus, as indicated earlier, the stochastic Ehrenfest equations only approximately hold for probability distributions of suitably narrow width. These features have interesting implications for the study of the classical limit of quantum theories and the role of the quantum Ehrenfest equations as a guide to the classical point particle as opposed to stochastic limit.

4.5 Stochastic Harmonic Oscillator

Let us then return to our favourite mechanical example of the simple harmonic oscillator only in stochastic form. Physically we could think of the system as being given by an ensemble of oscillators with a statistical distribution over the initial conditions.

Assume initial conditions are set by a probability density function $\rho_0(q_0, p_0, 0)$ and the standard Hamiltonian of the $H = \frac{q^2}{2m} + \frac{1}{2}kq^2$ as per the analysis of Section 3.4. The Liouville's equation (4.18) then gives us a homogenous first order PDE of the form:

$$\left[\frac{\partial}{\partial t} + \frac{p}{m}\frac{\partial}{\partial q} - 2kq\frac{\partial}{\partial p}\right]\rho(q,p,t) = 0 \tag{4.32}$$

Let us solve the equation by the method of characteristics. That is, we look for a solution of the form $\rho(q(s), p(s), t(s))$ where $(q(s), p(s), t(s))$ is a characteristic curve. Applying the total derivative gives us:

$$\frac{d}{ds}\rho(q(s), p(s), t(s)) = \frac{\partial \rho}{\partial q}\frac{dq}{ds} + \frac{\partial \rho}{\partial p}\frac{dp}{ds} + \frac{\partial \rho}{\partial t}\frac{dt}{ds} \tag{4.33}$$

which means we have the system of ODEs

$$\frac{dt}{ds} = 1 \tag{4.34}$$

$$\frac{dq}{ds} = \frac{p}{m} \tag{4.35}$$

$$\frac{dp}{ds} = -2kq \tag{4.36}$$

and recover the PDE via:

$$\frac{d}{ds}\rho(q(s), p(s), t(s)) = \left[\frac{\partial}{\partial t} + \frac{p}{m}\frac{\partial}{\partial q} - 2kq\frac{\partial}{\partial p}\right]\rho(q(s), p(s), t(s))$$
$$= 0$$

Setting $t(s = 0) = 0$ means we have that $t = s$ and our system reduces to:

$$\frac{dq}{dt} = \frac{p}{m} \tag{4.37}$$

$$\frac{dp}{dt} = -2kq \tag{4.38}$$

We already saw in Section 3.4 that if the initial position and momentum are q_0 and p_0 then this system is solved by the general solutions:

$$q(t) = q_0 \cos(\omega t) + \frac{p_0}{\sqrt{mk}} \sin(\omega t) \tag{4.39}$$

$$p(t) = -m\omega q_0 \sin(\omega t) + p_0 \cos(\omega t) \tag{4.40}$$

for $\omega = \sqrt{k/m}$. We want to use the same dynamical equations to infer the initial state from the present state and so we need to put in the initial state as (q,p) and run the equations back by $-t$ to get:

$$q_0 = q \cos(\omega t) - \frac{p}{\sqrt{mk}} \sin(\omega t) \tag{4.41}$$

$$p_0 = +m\omega q \sin(\omega t) + p \cos(\omega t) \tag{4.42}$$

Thus we have that:

$$\rho(q,p,t) = \rho_0(q\cos(\omega t) - \frac{p}{\sqrt{mk}}\sin(\omega t), m\omega q \sin(\omega t) + p\cos(\omega t)) \tag{4.43}$$

Let us then consider an initial probability distribution that is a Gaussian in position and momentum and thus we have that:

$$\rho_0(q_0,p_0) = \frac{1}{2\pi} e^{-[(q_0-X_0)^2 + p_0^2]/2} \tag{4.44}$$

where X_0 is an initial position offset. The equation for $\rho(q,p,t)$ then takes the form:

$$\rho(q,p,t) = \frac{1}{2\pi} e^{-[(q\cos(t)-p\sin(t)-X_0)^2]} \times \frac{1}{2\pi} e^{-[(q\sin(\omega t)+p\cos(t))^2]/2} \tag{4.45}$$

where we have set $\omega = k = m = 1$. The characteristic oscillatory motion of the system is now reflected in the motion of the Gaussian wave-packet in phase space as shown in Figure 3.

4.6 Further Topics of Study

- The Fokker-Planck Equation (Risken, 1996)
- Chaotic Stochastic Dynamics (Leith, 1996)
- Time Reversal Symmetry in Open Classical Systems (Guff & Rocco, 2023).

Classical and Quantum Phase Space Mechanics 39

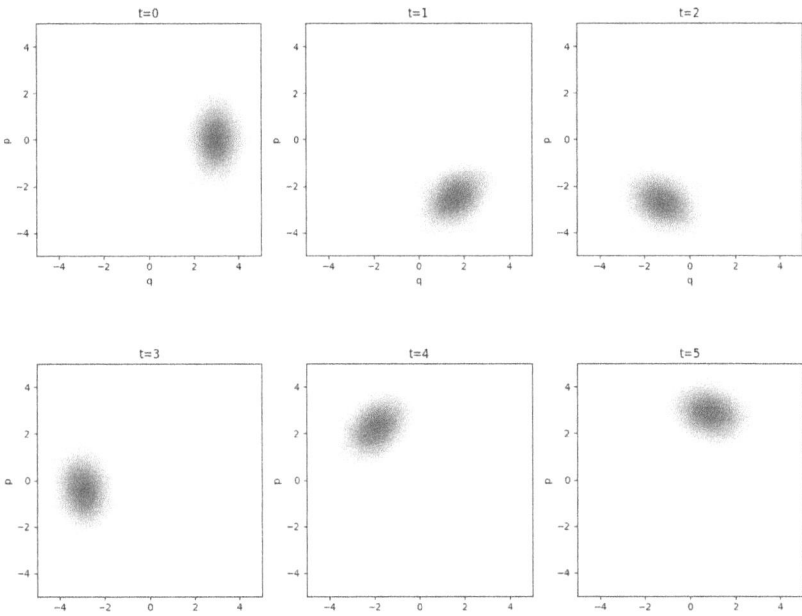

Figure 3 Graphs of Equation (4.45) showing successive time steps of a probability density function on phase space $\rho(q,p,t)$ that is initially Gaussian in position and momentum and evolves according to the Liouville equation with a simple harmonic potential. Generated using *Python* and *ChatGPT*.

5 Dissipation and Contact Phase Space Mechanics

> Contact geometry is the odd-dimensional twin of symplectic geometry. The relation between them is similar to the relation between projective and affine geometry.
>
> (Arnold & Givental, 2001, p.71)

5.1 Contact Geometry and Contact Hamiltonian Systems

Contact geometry is the odd-dimensional counterpart of symplectic geometry. In this section we will analyse the dynamical application of contact geometry to the class of contact Hamiltonian systems which extend the notion of a (symplectic) Hamiltonian dynamical system defined in the last section. The focus of this section is to set out the core formal ideas and, in particular, make explicit the analogy with the structure of symplectic mechanics as articulated in Section 3.1. For the most part we will follow (Arnold & Givental, 2001, §4) and Bravetti, Cruz, and Tapias (2017). Section 5.2 will focus on the feature of volume form non-conservation that marks a significant difference between symplectic and contact Hamiltonian system and provides a natural geometric framework for the representation of dissipation.

We define a *field of hyperplanes* on a smooth manifold when, in the tangent space to every point, we define a hyperplane that depends smoothly on the point. A field of hyperplanes can be defined locally by a non-vanishing differential 1-form η. That is, for a smooth manifold M we have that $\alpha|_x \neq 0$ for every point $x \in M$. A field of hyperplanes on a $(2n+1)$ dimension manifold is a *contact structure* if we have a $(2n+1)$-form such that:

$$\eta \wedge (d\eta)^n|_x \neq 0 \tag{5.1}$$

A manifold equipped with contact structure is a *contact manifold* or contact geometry, which we can indicate by a pair (M, η). In addition to the characteristic 1-form, η, a contact manifold possess a characteristic vector field which is the unique *Reeb vector field*, ξ, and defined by the conditions:

$$\iota_\xi \eta = 1 \tag{5.2}$$
$$\iota_\xi d\eta = 0 \tag{5.3}$$

The local analysis is particularly instructive. In the neighbourhood of each point of a $(2n+1)$-dimensional contact manifold, Darboux's theorem implies there will exist coordinates $(z, q_1 \ldots q_n, p_1 \ldots p_n)$ in which the contact structure has the form:

$$\eta = dz - p_i dq^i \tag{5.4}$$

In Darboux coordinate the Reeb vector field takes the simple form:

$$\xi = \frac{\partial}{\partial z} \tag{5.5}$$

There is thus is a natural geometric relation between the Reeb vector field and the 'odd' coordinate z owing to the fact that the Reeb vector picks out a 'vertical' direction with respect to the kernel of η.

We can use the contact structure on a given contact manifold to associate to every differentiable function on the manifold, $\mathcal{H}$, a *contact Hamiltonian vector field* which is generate by $\mathcal{H}$ via the relations:

$$\mathcal{L}_{X_\mathcal{H}} \eta = -\xi(\mathcal{H}) \eta \tag{5.6}$$
$$-\mathcal{H} = \iota_{X_\mathcal{H}} \eta \tag{5.7}$$

where $\xi(\mathcal{H})$ is the function given by acting on the contact Hamiltonian with the Reeb vector field and $\mathcal{H}$ is called the *contact Hamiltonian*. The first condition (5.6) implies that $X_\mathcal{H}$ leaves the contact form invariant up to a conformal factor (as discussed in Section 5.3 this means it generates a 'contactomorphism'). The second condition (5.7) implies that $X_{\mathcal{H}}$ is generated by a Hamiltonian function. In terms of Darboux coordinates we can re-write (5.6) as:

$$\mathcal{L}_{X_{\mathcal{H}}}\eta = -\frac{\partial \mathcal{H}}{\partial z}\eta \tag{5.8}$$

which will be useful later.

The two conditions can be used to study the behaviour of the contact form along the flow defined by a contact vector field. In particular, application of Cartan's magic formula gives us:

$$\mathcal{L}_{X_{\mathcal{H}}}\eta = \iota_{X_{\mathcal{H}}}d\eta + d(\iota_{X_{\mathcal{H}}}\eta) \tag{5.9}$$

Then, combined with the application of the exterior derivative to (5.7), we have that:

$$-d\mathcal{H} = d(\iota_{X_{\mathcal{H}}}\eta) = \mathcal{L}_{X_{\mathcal{H}}}\eta - \iota_{X_{\mathcal{H}}}d\eta \tag{5.10}$$

which in turn implies that:

$$d\mathcal{H} = \iota_{X_{\mathcal{H}}}d\eta - \mathcal{L}_{X_{\mathcal{H}}}\eta \tag{5.11}$$

This is in contrast to the symplectic case where writing things in terms of the symplectic potential we have by definition that:

$$dH = \iota_{X_H}d\theta \tag{5.12}$$

The contrast between these formulas expresses the fundamental difference between a Hamiltonian vector field, X_H on a symplectic manifold, $(M, d\theta)$ and a contact Hamiltonian vector field, $X_{\mathcal{H}}$ on a contact manifold, (M, η): *the characteristic 1-form is by preserved along the symplectic Hamiltonian flow of the first but not the contact Hamiltonian flow.*

The comparison between the Hamiltonian and contact Hamiltonian systems is made even more explicit in Darboux coordinates where we can write the contact Hamiltonian vector field out explicitly in components as:

$$X_{\mathcal{H}} = \left(p_i\frac{\partial \mathcal{H}}{\partial p_i}\right)\frac{\partial}{\partial z} - \left(p_i\frac{\partial \mathcal{H}}{\partial z} + \frac{\partial \mathcal{H}}{\partial q^i}\right)\frac{\partial}{\partial p_i} + \left(\frac{\partial \mathcal{H}}{\partial p_i}\right)\frac{\partial}{\partial q^i} \tag{5.13}$$

which implies that the flow of $X_{\mathcal{H}}$ has the form:

$$\dot{q}^i = \frac{\partial \mathcal{H}}{\partial p_i} \tag{5.14}$$

$$\dot{p}_i = -p_i\frac{\partial \mathcal{H}}{\partial z} - \frac{\partial \mathcal{H}}{\partial q^i} \tag{5.15}$$

$$\dot{z} = p_i\frac{\partial \mathcal{H}}{\partial p_i} \tag{5.16}$$

The correspondence with Hamilton's equations can be immediately recognised. In particular, when $\mathcal{H}$ does not depend upon z the first two equations *are* Hamilton's equations. Given this, it is not surprising that one can think of a contact Hamiltonian system in terms of a collection of symplectic Hamiltonian systems arranged as leaves of a foliation along the z direction.

5.2 Dissipation

Consider a contact Hamiltonian system $(M, \eta, \mathcal{H})$ and a smooth function on this space $\mathcal{F} \in C^\infty(M)$. The time evolution of $\mathcal{F}$ with respect to the parameter defined by the Hamiltonian vector field $X_\mathcal{H}$ is given an expression in Darboux coordinates that takes the form:

$$\frac{d\mathcal{F}}{dt} = X_\mathcal{H} \mathcal{F} \tag{5.17}$$

$$= -\mathcal{H}\frac{\partial \mathcal{F}}{\partial z} + p_i\left(\frac{\partial \mathcal{F}}{\partial z}\frac{\partial \mathcal{H}}{\partial p_i} - \frac{\partial \mathcal{F}}{\partial p_i}\frac{\partial \mathcal{H}}{\partial z}\right) + \left(\frac{\partial \mathcal{F}}{\partial q^i}\frac{\partial \mathcal{H}}{\partial p_i} - \frac{\partial \mathcal{F}}{\partial p_i}\frac{\partial \mathcal{H}}{\partial q^i}\right) \tag{5.18}$$

$$= -\mathcal{H}\frac{\partial \mathcal{F}}{\partial z} + p_i\left(\frac{\partial \mathcal{F}}{\partial z}\frac{\partial \mathcal{H}}{\partial p_i} - \frac{\partial \mathcal{F}}{\partial p_i}\frac{\partial \mathcal{H}}{\partial z}\right) + \{\mathcal{F}, \mathcal{H}\} \tag{5.19}$$

which is the contact Hamiltonian analogue of (3.20). We can thus understand the evolution of a contact Hamiltonian system in terms of a Poisson bracket evolution component together with contact corrections.

A function $\mathcal{F} \in C^\infty(M)$ is invariant under the contact Hamiltonian dynamics associated with $X_\mathcal{H}$ if it is constant along the flow of $X_\mathcal{H}$. Now consider the contact Hamiltonian function itself. We have immediately from equation (5.17) that the evolution of the Hamiltonian function is given by:

$$\frac{d\mathcal{H}}{dt} = -\mathcal{H}\frac{\partial \mathcal{H}}{\partial z} \tag{5.20}$$

This implies that $\mathcal{H}$ is invariant under the contact Hamiltonian dynamics if and only if $\mathcal{H} = 0$ or $\mathcal{H}$ does not depend upon z (where the or is non-exclusive). In the latter case we would then have an invariant Hamiltonian function $\mathcal{H} = H(q^i, p_i)$ which we can identify with the mechanical energy which is conserved by the contact dynamics. Thus, we have that a special case of contact Hamiltonian mechanics can be used to represent systems that are non-dissipative system or *mechanically conservative*.

Let us then consider a more general case in which the contact Hamiltonian takes the form:

$$\mathcal{H} = H(q^i, p_i) + h(z) \tag{5.21}$$

where we again interpret $H(q^i, p_i)$ as the mechanical energy. From (5.17) we have the function $H(q^i, p_i)$ has evolution equation:

$$\frac{dH}{dt} = -p_i \frac{\partial H}{\partial p_i} \frac{\partial h}{\partial z} \qquad (5.22)$$

The structure of this equation provides a physical basis to interpret $h(z)$ as a potential that generates a dissipative force. Typically this is understood in terms of an interaction with an external environment. We will consider the paradigmatic example of a dissipative system in terms of a linearly damped oscillator in Section 5.4.

5.3 Contactomorphisms

Recall once more that diffeomorphisms are invertible C^∞-mappings between the manifolds: $\varphi : M \to N$. Let us consider a pair of $(2n + 1)$-dimensional contact manifolds, (M, η) and (N, ν). If the push-forward of the diffeomorphism φ leaves the contact form invariant *up to a conformal factor*, so we have that $\tilde{\eta} = f\eta$, then the diffeomorphism is called a *contactomorphism*. Abstractly speaking, *contactomorphisms are the isomorphism of the category of contact manifolds*.[4]

Here we should note the contrast with symplectomorphisms which leave the symplectic form invariant exactly. The key feature behind this difference is that the *structure* of a contact geometry is only defined up to a conformal factor and thus there is a formal sense in which a given contact manifold, (M, η), is defined only up to contactomorphism.

The existence of a conformal factor in the contactomorphism transformation has an obvious implication for the behaviour of the contact volume form. In particular, while symplectomorphisms are such that they preserve the symplectic volume form, Ω_ω, contactomorphisms are such that they induce a *re-scaling* of the contact volume form:

$$\Omega_\eta = \eta \wedge (d\eta)^n \qquad (5.23)$$

We can see the explicit form of this re-scaling by considering the induced transformation on the two form $d\eta$ since we have that $d\tilde{\eta} = df \wedge \eta + f d\eta$ which implies that:

$$\tilde{\eta} \wedge (d\tilde{\eta})^n = f^{n+1} \wedge (d\eta)^n. \qquad (5.24)$$

Thus, we have that a contactomorphisms re-scales the volume form of a contact manifold by a term f^{n+1}. The re-scaling admits the special case in which

---

[4] Strictly speaking contactomorphisms include both time-independent and time-dependent contact transformations that leaves the contact form invariant up to a conformal factor. For our purpose it is sufficient to consider the time-independent case only. For discussion of time-dependent contact transformations see (Bravetti et al., 2017, 3.4).

Table 1 Contact mechanics is the odd-dimensional counterpart to symplectic mechanics.

Geometric Mechanics Comparison Table	
Symplectic Mechanics	**Contact Mechanics**
$2n$-dimension symplectic manifold	$2n+1$ dimension contact manifold
Hamiltonian System (M, H, ω)	Contact Hamiltonian System $(M, \mathcal{H}, \eta)$
Symplectic Potential $\theta = p_i dq^i$	Contact form $\eta = dz - p_i dq^i$
Volume Form $\Omega_\omega = d\theta^n$	Contact Volume Form $\Omega_\eta = \eta \wedge (d\eta)^n$
Hamilton's Equations $dH = \iota_{X_H} d\theta$	Contact Hamilton's Equations $d\mathcal{H} = \iota_{X_\mathcal{H}} d\eta - \mathcal{L}_{X_\mathcal{H}} \eta$
Liouville's theorem $\mathcal{L}_{X_H} \Omega_\omega = 0$	Volume Form Non-Conservation $\mathcal{L}_{X_\mathcal{H}} \Omega_\eta = -(n+1)\frac{\partial \mathcal{H}}{\partial z} \Omega_\eta$

$f = 1$ and thus the contact volume form is preserved. This corresponds to a symplectomorphism of the $2n$ symplectic manifold with Darboux coordinates (q, p).

We can then consider the behaviour of the contact volume form under the flow generated by a contact Hamiltonian vector field $X_\mathcal{H}$ by calculating the Lie derivative $\mathcal{L}_{X_\mathcal{H}}(\eta \wedge (d\eta)^n)$. Application of the product rule for the Lie derivative of the wedge product combined with Equation (5.9) then imply an expression of the form:

$$\mathcal{L}_{X_\mathcal{H}}(\eta \wedge (d\eta)^n) = -(n+1)\frac{\partial \mathcal{H}}{\partial z}(\eta \wedge (d\eta)^n) \tag{5.25}$$

We thus have non-conservation (compression or expansion) of the volume form under the contact Hamiltonian flow with the divergence taking the form:

$$\text{div}(X_\mathcal{H}) = -(n+1)\frac{\partial \mathcal{H}}{\partial z} \tag{5.26}$$

This corresponds to the failure of Liouville's theorem and provides the foundation for a statistical mechanical representation of dissipation in contact Hamiltonian systems to complement the loss of mechanical energy representation of dissipation we noted earlier. The comparison between symplectic and contact Hamiltonian systems is summarised in Table 1.

5.4 Damped Harmonic Oscillator

Let us consider a simple physical example of a contact Hamiltonian system that is the direct analogue of the Harmonic Oscillator we studied in Section 3.4.

We follow the treatment of (Bravetti, de León, Marrero, & Padrón, 2020, §2). It will prove instructive to consider a generic spatially dependent potential $V(q)$ and then specialise to the oscillator $V(q) = \frac{1}{2}q^2$ later. We set all constants to 1.

Consider a product manifold $\mathcal{C} = \mathbb{R} \times T^*\mathbb{R}^2$ with contact structure $\eta = dz - p_1 dq^1 - p_2 dq^2$. The contact Hamiltonian $\mathcal{H} : \mathcal{C} \to \mathbb{R}$ is:

$$\mathcal{H}(z, p, q) = \frac{1}{2}(p_1^2 + p_2^2) + V(q) + \gamma z \qquad (5.27)$$

with $\gamma \in \mathbb{R} - \{0\}$. This is equivalent to the case of $H(q^i, p_i) = \frac{1}{2}(p_1^2 + p_2^2) + V(q)$ and $h(z) = \gamma z$ in (5.21). The contact Hamilton equations are then given by:

$$\dot{q}^i = p_i \qquad (5.28)$$

$$\dot{p}^i = -\frac{\partial V}{\partial q^i} - \gamma p_i \qquad (5.29)$$

$$\dot{z} = (p_1^2 + p_2^2) - \mathcal{H} \qquad (5.30)$$

Correspondence to the standard Newtonian treatment of the damped oscillator is straightforward to establish. In particular, combining the first two equations gives the characteristic second-order equation:

$$\ddot{q}^i = -\gamma \dot{q}^i - \frac{\partial V}{\partial q^i} = 0 \qquad (5.31)$$

which is Newton's second law supplemented with a velocity-dependent damping force as expected.

Let us then specialise to the case of the one-dimensional damped oscillator with $V(q) = \frac{1}{2}q^2$ and $i = 1$ and $\gamma = 1$. The first two equations then have the characteristic form:

$$\dot{q} = p \qquad (5.32)$$

$$\dot{p} = -q - p \qquad (5.33)$$

This means that if we set $z = $ constant the contact Hamiltonian vector field takes the characteristic form of an (underdamped) oscillator. With $q(t) = e^{-t}\cos(t)$ and $p(t) = e^{-t}\sin(t)$. The geometric form of this vector field is illustrated in Figure 5. The full-contact Hamiltonian vector field is then given by supplementing equations (5.32) and (5.33) with the equation:

$$\dot{z} = \frac{1}{2}p^2 - \frac{1}{2}q^2 - z \qquad (5.34)$$

The full-contact Hamiltonian vector field of the system is depicted in Figure 4 together with the surfaces of constant z which reproduce the two-dimensional structure depicted in Figure 5.

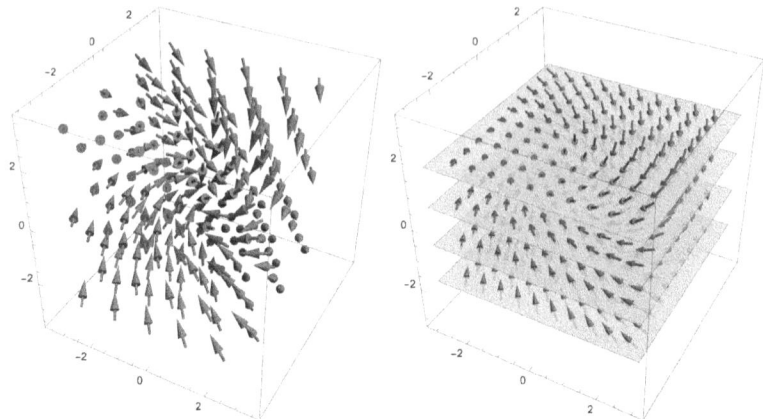

Figure 4 Illustration of the contact Hamiltonian vector field of an underdamped oscillator system. Left diagram shows the full vector field. Right diagram shows the vector field over slices of $z = $ constant. Generated with *Mathematica*

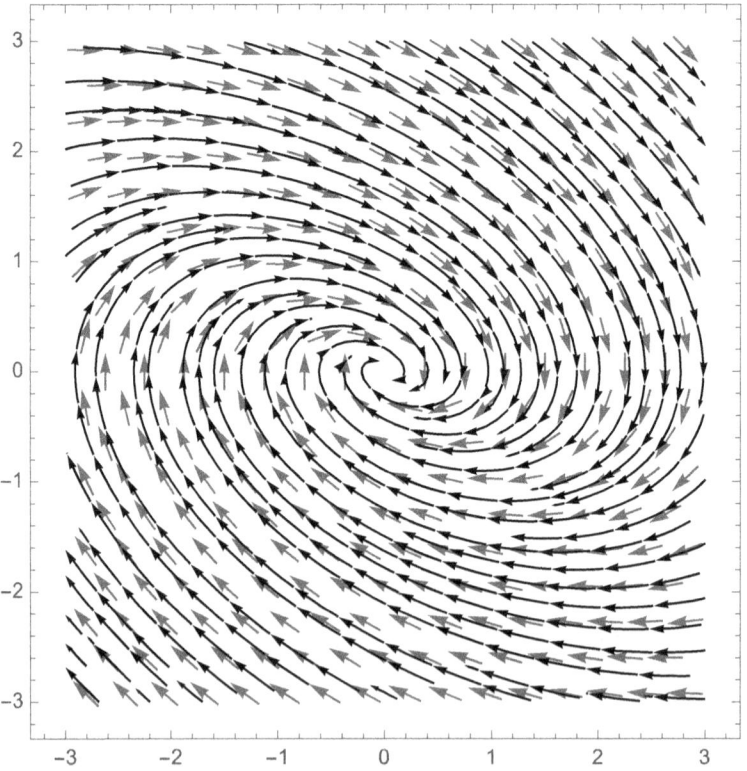

Figure 5 Phase portrait showing the contact Hamiltonian vector field and corresponding integral curves of an underdamped simple harmonic oscillator for a specific set of parameter values and $z = $ constant. Generated with *Mathematica*

5.5 Further Topics of Study

- Extended Phase Space as a Contact Manifold (Arnol'd, 2013; Gryb & Thébault, 2023).
- General Contact Hamiltonian Framework (Arnold & Givental, 2001; Bravetti et al., 2017; Bravetti & Tapias, 2015).
- Contact Reduction and Scaling Symmetry (Bravetti, Jackman, & Sloan, 2023).

6 Quasi-Probability and Quantum Phase Space Mechanics

> [M]any physicists hold the conviction that classical-valued position and momentum variables should not be simultaneously employed in any meaningful formula expressing quantum behaviour, simply because this would also seem to violate the uncertainty principle. However, they are wrong. Quantum mechanics *can* be consistently and autonomously formulated in phase space, with c-number position and momentum variables simultaneously placed on an equal footing, in a way that fully respects Heisenberg's principle. This other quantum framework is equivalent to both the Hilbert space approach and the path integral formulation. Quantum mechanics in phase space thereby gives a third point of view which provides still more insight and understanding.
>
> (Curtright, Fairlie, & Zachos, 2013, p.6)

6.1 Quasi-Measures and Quasi-Probability Densities

In this section we will consider the abstract generalisation of the probability density function in terms of a quasi-probability density. This abstract notion of a quasi-probability density will provide us with a formal foundation to introduce the Wigner function which is the privileged quasi-probability density densities used in quantum phase space mechanics. We will assume the formal details from measure theory already introduced in Section 4.1, and the reader may wish to refer back to that material in reading the following.

Let us begin by considering an a generalisation of a σ-algebra via the weaker notion of an *event algebra*. Here we are using a slight generalisation of the framework set out in Dowker and Wilkes (2022). In general the quasi-probability functions we will consider satisfy the stronger structure of being a finite-signed measure over a σ-algebra.

Consider a sample space, Ω, define by a non-empty set. An event algebra, $\mathfrak{E}$, is then a non-empty collection of subsets of Ω such that:

1. $\Omega \setminus \alpha \in \mathfrak{E}$ for all $\alpha \in \mathfrak{E}$ (closed under comemplementation);
2. $\alpha \cup \beta \in \mathfrak{E}$ for all $\alpha, \beta \in \mathfrak{E}$ (closed under finite union);

By definition we have that $\emptyset \in \mathfrak{E}$, $\Omega \in \mathfrak{E}$, and $\mathfrak{E}$ is closed under-finite intersection. We can then define a *quasi-probability model* as a triple $(\Omega, \mathfrak{E}, \tilde{\mu})$ where the three elements are a sample space, an event algebra, and a *quasi-measure* $\tilde{\mu}$ which is a set function $\tilde{\mu} : \mathfrak{E} \to \mathbb{R}$ which is such that $\tilde{\mu}(\Omega) = 1$ (normalised).

Two important features that a quasi-probability model does not have are σ-additivity and positivity. The first is since we have not insisted that the event algebra $\mathfrak{E}$ is a σ-algebra; it need not be closed under countable unions.[5] The second is since we have not insisted that the quasi-measure $\tilde{\mu}$ is a measure; it need not be positive (nor indeed σ-additive). Strengthening the model to include these features results in the familiar formal structure of a classical probability model.

In parallel to the idea of a quasi-measure we can consider a quasi-probability density function. This is a function that induces a quasi-measure in a manner analogous the way in which a probability density function induces a probability measure. Assuming already that we are in a phase space representation where the space $\mathbb{R}^{2N}$ is equipped with the usual symplectic chart (q, p) and an integration measure $dqdp$ we can introduce the a *quasi-probability density function* as a function $F : \mathbb{R}^{2N} \to \mathbb{R}$ that induces a quasi-measure $\tilde{\mu}$ such that:

$$\tilde{\mu}(C) = \int_C F(q,p) d^N q d^N p \tag{6.1}$$

for some collections of sub-regions of the state space $C \subset \mathbb{R}^{2N}$ and the normalisation can be defined via the condition:

$$\tilde{\mu}(\Gamma) = \lim_{n \to \infty} \int_{B_n} F(q,p) dqdp = 1 \tag{6.2}$$

where $B_n = \{(q,p) \mid |q|^2 + |p|^2 \leq r_n\}$ and $\lim_{n \to \infty} r_n = \infty$ (Aniello, 2016). The role of the limits in (6.2) are crucial. In particular, they impose a weaker condition of normalisation that is compatible with the *failure* of Lebesgue integrability.

Consider, in particular, the Wigner quasi-probability representation, to be discussed in more detail shortly. In this context, it can be proved that the

---

[5] For a detailed discussion of relationship between forms of additivity and classical and quantum probabilities see Arageorgis, Earman, and Ruetsche (2017).

relevant quasi-probability density function, the Wigner function, is *not necessarily* Lebesgue integrable (Daubechies, 1983) and thus that there exists $F(q,p)$ such that:

$$\tilde{\mu}(\mathbb{R}^{2N}) = \int_{\mathbb{R}^{2N}} |F(q,p)| \, d^N q \, d^N p \not< \infty \qquad (6.3)$$

One can show, however, that the Wigner function is an element of $L^2(T^\star\mathbb{R}) \cap C_0(T^\star\mathbb{R})$ and is thus a square integrable and continuous function on the phase space (Landsman, 2012, p. 142). Moreover, the induced quasi-measure is σ-additive and the Wigner function induces a *finite signed measure* (Dias, de Gosson, & Prata, 2019).

As noted in Dawid and Thébault (2025), a further important feature of the Wigner quasi-probability density function, W, is a restriction of the essential support to volumes of phase space greater than equal to one in units of $\hbar$ (Dell'Antonio, 2016, p.19). As noted in Section 4.1, the essential support of a function, ess sup(f), indicates the smallest closed subset in the domain of a measurable function such that the function can be zero 'almost' everywhere outside that subset. Significantly, the essential support of the Wigner function, ess sup(W), cannot be less than a characteristic volume of one in units of $\hbar$. We therefore have that, in contrast to the classical case, it is *not* possible to concentrate a Wigner quasi-probability density almost entirely at a single point. This amounts to precluding the possibility that the Wigner quasi-probability density function approximates a δ-function in phase space (Leonhardt, 2010, p.71). As such, phase space points are not in ess sup(W) and we cannot have a situation in which the Wigner function is non-zero at a point but zero (almost) everywhere else.

The bound on the Wigner function, of course, means that δ-functions not admissible quasi-probability density functions. Furthermore, due to the unit norm, the bound also means that any function that leads to localisation of the quasi-probably mass of order $\hbar$ are excluded. Physically speaking, these connections can be understood as a consequence of the Heisenberg uncertainty principle (in generalised Robertson–Schrödinger form) which, in turn, is a direct consequence of the non-commutative structure induced by the $\star$-product, see (Curtright et al., 2013, §5) and (Huggett, Lizzi, & Menon, 2021, §5.1). In particular, by the Cauchy–Schwarz inequality the Wigner function is bounded such that $-\frac{1}{\epsilon} \leq W(q,p) \leq \frac{1}{\epsilon}$ with $\epsilon = \frac{\hbar}{2}$. Significantly, the bound and the corresponding failure of the localisability of the Wigner function are independent from its negativity.

We will provide a more detailed presentation of the Wigner function in Section 6.3. In preparation for this discussion in the following Section 6.2, before we will provide an abstract characterisation of quantum phase space model to parallel the presentation of stochastic phase space models in Section 4.2.

6.2 Quantum Phase Space Models

Following, Dawid and Thébault (2025), a phase space representation of a quantum possibility space model is a triple is a triple $(\Gamma, \mathcal{O}, F)$ that takes the following form:

1. **State Space**: $\Gamma = \mathbb{R}^{2N}$ represents the space of possible states of system as a 2N-dimensional symplectic manifold equipped with the closed non-degenerate two form $\omega = dq \wedge dp$ and associated volume measure $dqdp$ in the Darboux chart;

2. **Observable Algebra**: $\mathfrak{A}$ represents observables as a (non-commutative) Moyal algebra of Weyl symbols which are the Wigner transforms of the algebra of (Weyl ordered) bounded linear operators $\mathcal{B}(\mathcal{H})$ on a Hilbert space of square integral functions $\mathcal{H} = L^2(\mathbb{R}^{2N})$. The binary operation is given by a $\star$-product operation which can be expressed as a pseudo-differential operator in powers of $\hbar$ and the non-commutativity of the algebra is expressed via the fundamental relation that $[\hat{A}, \hat{B}] = \{\{A, B\}\} \equiv \frac{1}{i\hbar}(A \star B - A \star B)$ for all $A, B \in \mathfrak{A}$ and all $\hat{A}, \hat{B} \in \mathcal{B}(\mathcal{H})$. The distinguished function $H \in \mathfrak{A}$ induces a time evolution automorphism via the Moyal bracket such that $\frac{d}{dt}A = \{\{A, H\}\}$ for all $A \in \mathfrak{A}$;

3. **Quasi-Probability Density Function**: is a possibility space weighting function $F(q, p) : \Gamma \to \mathbb{R}$ that induces a quasi-measure $\tilde{\mu}(B) = \int_B F(q, p) dqdp$ that satisfies the conditions:

   (a) $\tilde{\mu}(\Gamma) = \lim_{n \to \infty} \int_{\mathbf{B}_n} F(q, p) dqdp = 1$ where $\mathbf{B}_n = \{(q, p) \mid |q|^2 + |p|^2 \leq r_n\}$ (normalised)
   (b) $|F(q, p)| \leq \frac{1}{\epsilon}$ (bounded)
   (c) If $B_1, \ldots, B_n, \ldots \in \mathcal{B}$ with $B_i \cap B_j = \emptyset$ for $i \neq j$ then $\tilde{\mu}(\cup_{n=1}^{\infty} B_n) = \sum_{n=1}^{\infty} \int_{B_n} F(q, p) dqdp$ (σ-additive)

   where $B \in \mathcal{B}$ are the Borel sets $\mathcal{B}(\mathbb{R}^{2N})$

4. **Expectation Values**: $\langle A \rangle$ is the expectation value or mean of an observable defined as: $\langle A \rangle \equiv \int_\Gamma A(q, p) \star F(q, p) dqdp$ for all $A \in \mathfrak{A}$.

The model provides an interpretation (assignment of meaning) to a quasi-probability structure as follows: The state space Γ is the sample space Ω and the event algebra $\mathfrak{A}$ is given by regions of phase space of volume greater than or equal to some minimum volume which depends upon ϵ. The quasi-measure $\tilde{\mu}$ is given by the integral of the quasi-probability density function with respect to the volume measure.

6.3 The Wigner Function

The central formal object of the phase space formulation of quantum theory is the Wigner function, $W(q,p)$ (E. Wigner, 1932). The Wigner function is the most widely used quasi-probability distribution function on phase space. A concise and very clear introduction to the Wigner function and the quantum phase space formalism is Curtright et al. (2013). Further useful discussions can be found in Case 2008); De Gosson (2017) Hillery, O'Connell, Scully, and Wigner (1984); Leonhardt (2010); O'Connell and Wigner (1981). The small philosophical literature is principally consists of the discussions found in Cohen (1966); Friederich (2021); Sneed (1970); Suppes (1961); Wallace (2021). A concise formal overview which includes extension to non-canonical phase space variables can be found in Dubois, Saalmann, and Rost (2021).

The most general form of the Wigner function is in terms of a transformation of the density matrix operator $\hat{\rho}$ defined on some Hilbert space $\mathcal{H}$. Significantly, this presentation of the function is well defined for pure or mixed states. Explicitly, we write $W(q,p)$ as

$$W(q,p) = \frac{1}{2\pi} \int dq' \langle q - q' | \hat{\rho} | q + q' \rangle e^{-iq'p} \tag{6.4}$$

where q and p represent classical phase space position and momentum values.[6]

For a pure state with spatial wavefunction $\psi(q)$ we can provide a more explicit representation of the Wigner function as:

$$W_\psi(q,p) = \frac{1}{2\pi} \int dq' \, \psi^*\left(q - \frac{\hbar}{2}q'\right) e^{-iyp} \psi\left(q + \frac{\hbar}{2}q'\right) \tag{6.5}$$

For a normalised input wavefunctions it is normalised since we have that:

$$\int dp\,dq\, W_\psi(q,p) = 1 \tag{6.6}$$

The Wigner function does not privilege the spatial over momentum wavefunction. We can see this by considering the Fourier transform to the momentum-space wavefunction:

$$\phi = \int dq \, e^{\frac{iqp}{\hbar}} \psi(q) \frac{1}{\sqrt{2\pi\hbar}} \tag{6.7}$$

---

[6] Formally, the Wigner function is the symmetrically ordered complex Fourier transform of the characteristic function on the quantum phase space. For instructive explicit treatments in the context of Bosonic systems see Weedbrook et al. (2012) and Adesso, Ragy, and Lee (2014).

which leads to a symmetric expression for the Wigner function for momentum space wavefunction $\phi(p)$ with the roles of q and p switched:

$$W_\phi(q,p) = \frac{1}{2\pi} \int dp'\, \phi^*\left(p - \frac{\hbar'}{2}\right) e^{-ip'q} \phi\left(p + \frac{\hbar}{2}p'\right) \tag{6.8}$$

These expressions are for a pure state.

Among the quasi-probability distribution that we may define on phase space the Wigner function can be picked out based upon a particular symmetric operator ordering.[7] It can also be motivated on physical grounds. In particular, although Wigner originally proposed the choice of a function of the form (6.5), based upon simplicity considerations, he was later able to show that the Wigner function is implied uniquely by two overlapping subsets of conditions, each of which has a clear physical motivation. The conditions are:

1. *Real*. The Wigner function is a real function, $W_\psi(q,p) = \langle \psi | \hat{A}(q,p) | \psi \rangle$ for $\hat{A}(q,p)$ a self-adjoint operator depending upon q and p.
2. *Probability Shadow*. The p and q projections of the Wigner function lead to marginal probability distributions and the function is normalised; that is, we have that: i) $\int dp\, W_\psi(q,p) = |\psi(q)|^2$; ii) $\int dq\, W_\psi(q,p) = |\psi(p)|^2$; and iii) $\int dq\, dp\, W_\psi(q,p) = 1$
3. *Galilei Covariant*. The Wigner function should be Galilei covariant; that is, we have that if $\psi(q) \to \psi(q+a)$ then $W_\psi(q,p) \to W_\psi(q+a,p)$ and if $\psi(q) \to e^{ip'q/\hbar}\psi(q)$ then $W_\psi(q,p) \to W_\psi(q,p-p')$
4. *Reflection Covariant*. The Wigner function should be covariant under reflections in space and time; that is, if $\psi(q) \to \psi(-q)$ then $W_\psi(q,p) \to W_\psi(-q,-p)$ and if $\psi(q) \to \psi^*(q)$ then $W_\psi(q,p) \to W_\psi(q,-p)$
5. *Newtonian*. The Wigner function for the force-free case should recover the classical equation of motion; that is, we should have that:

$$\frac{\partial W_\psi}{\partial t} = -\frac{p}{m}\frac{\partial W_\psi}{\partial q} \tag{6.9}$$

6. *Overlap Integral*. The overlap between two wavefunctions can be expressed in terms of their Wigner functions as:

$$\left| \int dq\, \psi^*(q)\phi(q) \right|^2 = (2\phi\hbar) \int dq\, dp\, W_\psi(q,p) W_\phi(q,p) \tag{6.10}$$

The conditions 1–6 all have a physical motivation that could plausible be understood to come from our expectations regarding the empirical content of quantum physics and the need to recover the empirical content of classical

---

[7] See (Barnett & Radmore, 2002, §4) for discussion.

physics in the appropriate limit. The condition 6 implies that if ϕ and ψ are orthogonal then:

$$(2\phi\hbar)\int dq dp W_\psi(q,p) W_\phi(q,p) = 0 \tag{6.11}$$

which means that $W_\psi(q,p)$ cannot be everywhere positive. The uniqueness of the expression for the Wigner function of a pure state (6.5) then can be alternatively derived from the combination of 1–5 (E. Wigner, 1979) or from 1 to 4 and 6 (O'Connell & Wigner, 1981). These results can be generalised to the case of mixed states. Most significantly, it can be proved that any quasi-probability distribution function of the form $F(q,p) = \langle\psi|\hat{A}(q,p)|\psi\rangle$ which and reproduces the marginal probability densities cannot also be positive semi-definite (E. P. Wigner, 1971). Wigner negativity is evidently a distinctive non-classical feature of the Wigner function. The size of the regions of negativity in phase space are of order $\hbar$ which will be important in what follows. Significantly, the subset of Wigner functions that correspond to minimum uncertainty coherent states can be shown to be everywhere positive (and visa versa) (Hudson, 1974; Mariño, 2021).

Despite its negativity the Wigner function has a number of attractive features that mark it out as privileged among the quasi-probability distribution functions. In particular, the density and marginal features noted earlier crucially depend upon the $\star$-product associated to the Wigner function being the Moyal $\star$-product product. This is what allows one $\star$-product to be dropped inside an integral via integration by parts leading to formal behaviour that matches that of a genuine probability density function for the marginals and expectation values. This feature is in contrast to the Husimi Q-function for which the associated product $\circledast$ cannot be integrated out and leads to marginals distributions that do not correspond to those of quantum mechanics (Curtright et al., 2013, §13). Thus, although the Q-function is positive definite, it has features that make any potential connection with genuine probability densities much less direct. Moreover, as per our definition of a quasi-probability density function, both the Wigner function and the Q-function are bounded ($\epsilon = \pi$ for the Q-function) and thus cannot be concentrated (almost) entirely in at a single phase space point as per our earlier discussion. There is also the Glauber–Sudarshan P-function. This function, which can also be negative, is strictly not a quasi-probability density as per our definition since it is not bounded. Further, despite its usage in various areas of optics, the function is the most pathological member of the quasi-probability family and may fail to exist as a *well-tempered* distribution (Leonhardt, 2010, p. 82). As such, the Wigner function is certainly better placed to be the distinguished representation of quasi-probability.

6.4 The Weyl Transform and the Moyal Bracket

The transformation between the density matrix $\hat{\rho}$ and the Wigner function W can be generalised to an arbitrary operator $\hat{A}$ as:

$$A(q,p) = \frac{1}{2\pi} \int dq' \langle q - q' | \hat{A} | q + q' \rangle e^{-iq'p} \tag{6.12}$$

Where we understand $A(q,p)$ to be the *Weyl transform* for the operator $\hat{A}$. As such the Weyl transform coverts an operator on Hilbert space, with the preferred Weyl operator ordering, into a function on phase space.

An important property of the Weyl transform is that the trace of the product of two operators $\hat{A}$ and $\hat{B}$ is expressed in phase space in terms of the integral of the product of the relevant Weyl transforms:

$$\text{Tr}[\hat{A}\hat{B}] = \frac{1}{\hbar} \int \int A(q,p) B(q,p) dq dp \tag{6.13}$$

This immediately implies that we can express the expectation value of an operator as:

$$\langle A \rangle = \text{Tr}[\hat{\rho}\hat{B}] = \int \int W(q,p) A(q,p) dq dp \tag{6.14}$$

As such the Wigner function can be identified as the role of an analogous to a classical probability density in that we obtain the average value of a quantity by integrating over that quantity multiplied by the Wigner function. We know, of course, that the Wigner function is a quasi-probability density and thus we should not take the analogy at face value.

For simple operators that can be expressed as sums of $\hat{q}$ and $\hat{p}$ (i.e. do not have terms of the form $\hat{q}\hat{p}$ or $\hat{q}^2\hat{p}$) the Weyl transform returns the unmodified classical observable expression. We will see this in our treatment of the quantum oscillator in Section 6.6. In general, however, as noted, both the Wigner function in particular, and the Weyl transform in general, are defined in terms of a preferred operator ordering. For a general operator this means that the resolution of operator ordering ambiguities will introduce $\hbar$ quantum corrections to the phase space observables and thus the functions $A(q,p)$ cannot be simply equated with the observables of the classical Hamiltonian system. For more details see (Curtright et al., 2013, §12).

As we saw in at the end of Section 3.2, the observables of a classical Hamiltonian system form a Lie algebra with the Poisson bracket the associated Lie bracket. Similarly, the observables of a quantum system in the Hilbert space formalism also form a Lie algebra, and in this case the commutator is the associated Lie bracket. It is natural then to seek to define analogous structures in the quantum phase space formalism. In this context we define the *Moyal bracket* of two observables in the quantum phase space formalism as equivalent to the commutator of the corresponding operators under the Weyl transform. That is, we have that:

$$i\hbar[[A(q,p), B(q,p)]] \equiv [\hat{A}, \hat{B}] \tag{6.15}$$

The Moyal bracket is a Lie bracket and can be derived as the unique one-parameter ($\hbar$) associative *deformation* of the Poisson bracket.[8] Indeed, up to second order in $\hbar$ the Moyal bracket corresponds to the Poisson bracket (Dubois et al., 2021). We thus have that:

$$[[A, B]] = \{A, B\} + O(\hbar^2) \tag{6.16}$$

In order to provide an intrinsic expression for the Moyal bracket we can introduce the $\star$-product which takes the form:

$$\star \equiv \exp(\overleftarrow{\partial}_q \overrightarrow{\partial}_p - \overleftarrow{\partial}_p \overrightarrow{\partial}_q) \tag{6.17}$$

where the over arrows imply application of the partial derivative to the left-hand and right-hand side of the $\star$-product respectively. That is, we have that:

$$A(q,p)\overleftarrow{\partial}_q B(q,p) = \frac{\partial A(q,p)}{\partial q} B(q,p)$$

$$A(q,p)\overrightarrow{\partial}_q B(q,p) = A(q,p)\frac{\partial B(q,p)}{\partial p}$$

We can write the Moyal bracket in terms of the $\star$-product as:

$$i\hbar[[A(q,p), B(q,p)]] = A(q,p) \star B(q,p) - B(q,p) \star A(q,p) \tag{6.18}$$

The $\star$-product involves exponentials of derivative operators and in practice is most easily evaluated through translation of function arguments (Curtright et al., 2013, Lemma 1.):

$$A(q,p) \star B(q,p) = A\left(q + \frac{i\hbar}{2}\overrightarrow{\partial}_p, p - \frac{i\hbar}{2}\overrightarrow{\partial}_q\right) B(q,p) \tag{6.19}$$

This formulae is actually one representative of a general pattern of representations of the Moyal star product bidifferential operator expansions that takes the form:

$$(A \star B)(q,p) = A\left(q + \frac{i\hbar}{2}\overrightarrow{\partial}_p, p - \frac{i\hbar}{2}\overrightarrow{\partial}_q\right) B(q,p) \tag{6.20}$$

$$= A(q,p) B\left(q - \frac{i\hbar}{2}\overleftarrow{\partial}_p, p + \frac{i\hbar}{2}\overleftarrow{\partial}_q\right) \tag{6.21}$$

---

[8] For a foundational discussion that includes the related notion of deformation quantisation, see Feintzeig (2022).

$$= A\left(q + \frac{i\hbar}{2}\overrightarrow{\partial_p}, p\right) B\left(q - \frac{i\hbar}{2}\overleftarrow{\partial_p}, p\right) \tag{6.22}$$

$$= A\left(q, p - \frac{i\hbar}{2}\overrightarrow{\partial_q}\right) B\left(q, p + \frac{i\hbar}{2}\overleftarrow{\partial_q}\right). \tag{6.23}$$

Later we will find these expressions of particular use for explicitly calculating Moyal star products in mechanical examples.

It is also possible to write the ⋆-product in terms of a generalised convolution integral via the Fourier transform, see Baker (1958) and (Curtright et al., 2013, pp. 44-5). If there is only one ⋆-product involved we can recover the plain product as:

$$\int dpdq A \star B = \int dpdq A \star B = \int dq dp A B \tag{6.24}$$

Static Wigner functions can be shown to obey the ⋆-genvalue equation (Curtright et al., 2013, Lemma 3.):

$$H(q,p) \star W(q,p) = H\left(q + \frac{i\hbar}{2}\overrightarrow{\partial}_p, p - \frac{i\hbar}{2}\overrightarrow{\partial}_q\right) W(q,p) = EW(q,p) \tag{6.25}$$

where E is the energy eigenvalue of the time-independent Schrödinger equation, $\hat{H}\psi = E\psi$.

6.5 Moyal's Equation and Ehrenfest's Theorem

The basic dynamical equation for phase space quantum mechanics is *Moyal's equation* which expresses the rate of change of any observable $A(q,p)$ via the Moyal bracket as:

$$\frac{\partial A(q,p)}{\partial t} = \frac{1}{i\hbar}(H(q,p) \star A(q,p) - A(q,p) \star H(q,p)) \tag{6.26}$$

$$= [[H(q,p), A(q,p)]] \tag{6.27}$$

where $H(q,p)$ is the Weyl transform of the Hamiltonian operator $\hat{H}$. As noted, $H(q,p)$ will not in general be equivalent to the classical Hamiltonian function but will rather have order quantum corrections.

Applying Moyal's equation to the Wigner function $W(q,p)$ gives us an expression of the form:

$$\frac{\partial W(q,p)}{\partial t} = [[H(q,p), W(q,p)]] \tag{6.28}$$

$$= \{H(q,p), W(q,p)\} + O(\hbar^2) \tag{6.29}$$

Expressing things in this form allows an instructive comparison between the quantum and classical phase space formalisms. In particular, recall that the

Liouville equation for a classical probability density (4.18) took the form:

$$\frac{\partial \rho(q,p)}{\partial t} + \{\rho(q,p), H_{cl}(q,p)\} = 0 \tag{6.30}$$

where we have written the classical Hamiltonian function as $H_{cl}(q,p)$ for clarity. By contrast, for phase space quantum mechanics we have that

$$\frac{\partial W(q,p)}{\partial t} + \{W(q,p), H(q,p)\} = O(\hbar^2) \tag{6.31}$$

Thus the quantum correction terms express precisely the sense in which the Wigner function fails to behave like its classical counter part. In other words, quantum phase space representations encode the failure of classicality in terms of the failure of Liouville's theorem. In particular, we find that the $O(\hbar^2)$ higher momentum derivatives of the Wigner function that are present in the Moyal bracket, but absent in the Poisson bracket, modify the Liouville flow into characteristic quantum configurations (Curtright et al., 2013, p. 59).

A particularly beautiful visualisation of this way of thinking about the classical-quantum distinction comes from the interpretation of (quasi-)probability density as a phase space fluid flow. Whereas in the classical case Equation (4.18) means that the flow of the classical probability density $\rho(q,p)$ on phase space is interpreted in terms of the flow of a *incompressible fluid*, the contrasting Equation (6.28) means that the flow of the quantum quasi-probability density on phase space, $W(q,p)$ is interpreted in terms of the flow of a *compressible fluid*.

We can see this even more explicitly by considering an the flux integral for an arbitrary region Δ about some representative point in phase space:

$$\frac{d}{dt} \int_\Delta dq dp W = \int_\Delta dq dp \left(\frac{\partial W}{\partial t} + \partial_q(\dot{q}W) + \partial_p(\dot{p}W) \right) \tag{6.32}$$

$$= \int_\Delta dq dp \left([[H,W]] - \{H,W\} \right) \tag{6.33}$$

$$\neq 0 \tag{6.34}$$

In the vivid terms of Curtright et al. (2013) we thus find that 'the phase space region does not conserve in time the number of point swarming about the representative point: points diffuse away, in general, without maintaining the density of the quantum quasi-probability fluid; and, conversely they are not prevented form coming together, in contrast for deterministic flow behaviour' (p. 58). The quasi-probability density associated with regions of phase space thus manifests a *local violation of additivity over time* in marked contrast to the classical probability density function in phase space.

A further, and significant, application of Moyal's equation is to the recovery of semi-classical equations of motion. In particular, we can express the rate of change of the average of a time-independent quantum phase space function $A(q,p)$ as:

$$\frac{d\langle A \rangle}{dt} = \int dqdp \frac{\partial W}{\partial t} A \tag{6.35}$$

$$= \frac{1}{i\hbar} \int dqdp (H \star W - W \star H) \star A \tag{6.36}$$

$$= \frac{1}{i\hbar} \int dqdp W[[A,H]] \tag{6.37}$$

$$= \langle [[A,H]] \rangle \tag{6.38}$$

This is the general form of the Ehrenfest relation in the quantum phase space formalism.

Assuming that we have a Hamiltonian of the standard form, $H(q,p) = \frac{1}{2}p^2 + V(q)$, where all constants are set to 1, then we immediately get for the first two moments that:

$$\frac{d}{dt}\langle q \rangle = \langle [[q,H]] \rangle \tag{6.39}$$

$$\frac{d}{dt}\langle p \rangle = \langle [[p,V(q)]] \rangle \tag{6.40}$$

Consider the second equation. To compute the relevant brackets we just need the identity:

$$[[p,F(q)]] = -\frac{dF(q)}{dq} \tag{6.41}$$

This holds for any polynomial function $F(q)$ and can be straightforwardly derived by application of the Bopp shift formulas (6.20) and (6.21) (or equivalently via the Taylor expansions).

Applying (6.41) for $A = p$ in (6.35) immediately gives us:

$$\frac{d\langle p \rangle}{dt} = \frac{1}{2}\langle [[p,p^2]] \rangle + \langle [[p,V(q)]] \rangle \tag{6.42}$$

$$= \langle [[p,V(q)]] \rangle \tag{6.43}$$

$$= -\left\langle \frac{dV(q)}{dq} \right\rangle \tag{6.44}$$

This is, of course, simply to recover Hamilton's second equation (which is a form of Newton's second law) as a semi-classical equation for the first moments. Moreover, it is precisely the same formula as we derived for the first momentum moment in stochastic Ehrenfest relation (4.25) in Section 4.4.

More interestingly, as per our earlier discussion, we find that the average position and the average momentum in the quantum phase space formalism will follow a classical trajectory only if we have that:

$$\left\langle \frac{dV(q)}{dq} \right\rangle \approx \frac{dV(\langle q \rangle)}{dq} \tag{6.45}$$

In this sense we find that the approximate limiting relation is between stochastic phase space and quantum phase space formalism. The classical deterministic phase space theory may fail to be even approximately recovered for suitably wide distributions or whenever the higher-order moments become relevant.

This highlights the idea articulated in Ballentine and McRae (1998) that the classical limit of a quantum theory is not a single deterministic classical trajectory in phase space, but an ensemble of trajectories in a stochastic phase space. In particular, the averages and higher moments of the quantum and classical distributions can agree in situations where neither is approximately obeying Newton's laws for deterministic evolution.

6.6 Quantum Harmonic Oscillator

Let us conclude our discussion by returning to our old friend the one-dimensional simple harmonic oscillator. We again have a Hamiltonian of the form:

$$H(q,p) = \frac{1}{2}\left(q^2 + p^2\right) \tag{6.46}$$

where we have set $k = m = 1$ for convenience. Evidently there is no operator ordering ambiguity so we can use the classical expression for the Hamiltonian in the quantum phase space formalism.

Application of the $\star$-genvalue equation (6.25) gives us:

$$\left(\left(q + \frac{i\hbar}{2}\partial_p\right)^2 + \left(p - \frac{i\hbar}{2}\partial_q\right)^2 - 2E\right)W(q,p) = 0 \tag{6.47}$$

Taking the imaginary part of this equation gives us an expression of the form:

$$(q\partial_p - p\partial_q)W(q,p) = 0 \tag{6.48}$$

which implies we can restrict W to a function $W(z)$ depending upon a phase space scalar $z = \frac{4}{\hbar}H = \frac{2}{\hbar}(q^2 + p^2)$.

The real part of the $\star$-genvalue equation then gives us:

$$\left(\frac{z}{4} - z\partial_z^2 - \partial_z - \frac{E}{\hbar}\right)W(z) = 0 \tag{6.49}$$

which we can solve with an ansatz $W(z) = e^{\frac{-z}{2}} L(z)$ where $L(z)$ is the Laguerre polynomial:

$$L_n = \frac{1}{n!} e^z \partial_z^n (e^{-z} z^n) \tag{6.50}$$

The $\star$-genvalue functions for the simple harmonic oscillator are given by:

$$W_n = \frac{(-1)^2}{\pi \hbar} e^{-2H/\hbar} L_n\left(\frac{4H}{\hbar}\right) \tag{6.51}$$

The first three $\star$-genvalue functions are graphed in Figure 6.[9] Further analysis of this model can be found in (Curtright et al., 2013, §7).

Let us then derive the Ehrenfest relation in the quantum phase space formalisms for the first moments. From (6.35) we have that:

$$\frac{d\langle A \rangle}{dt} = \langle [[A, H]] \rangle \tag{6.52}$$

$$= \frac{1}{2} \langle [[A, q^2]] \rangle + \frac{1}{2} \langle [[A, p^2]] \rangle \tag{6.53}$$

For $A = q$ we have:

$$\frac{d\langle q \rangle}{dt} = \frac{1}{2i\hbar} \int dq dp W[[q, p^2]] \tag{6.54}$$

$$= \int dq dp W p \tag{6.55}$$

$$= \langle p \rangle \tag{6.56}$$

where we have used the relations that $[[q, p^2]] = [[q,p]] \star p + p \star [[q,p]]$ and $[[q,p]] = i\hbar$.

Applying (6.41) for $A = p$ means in case of the quantum Harmonic oscillator we get:

$$\frac{d\langle p \rangle}{dt} = -\langle q \rangle \tag{6.57}$$

Combining (6.54) and (6.57) gives us the characteristic ODE for a Harmonic oscillator expressed in terms of the first moments of position:

$$\frac{d^2 \langle q \rangle}{dt^2} = -\langle q \rangle \tag{6.58}$$

6.7 Further Topics of Study

- Wigner Negativity, Contextuality and Entanglement (Booth, Chabaud, & Emeriau, 2022; Okay, Bermejo-Vega, Browne, & Raussendorf, 2017).

---

[9] Credit Samira Bahrami (2011), "Wigner Function of Harmonic Oscillator" Wolfram Demonstrations Project. demonstrations.wolfram.com/WignerFunctionOfHarmonicOscillator/

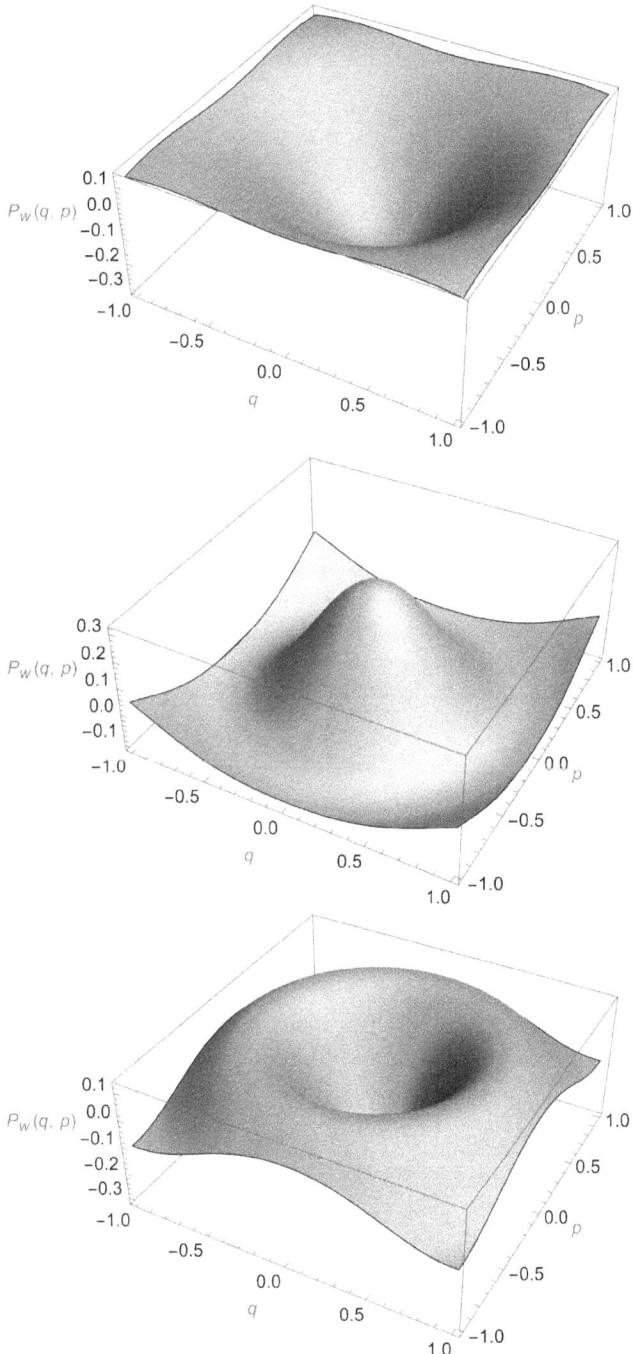

Figure 6 Wigner $\star$-genvalue function $P_{W_n}(q,p)$ for the simple harmonic oscillator for $n = 1, 2, 3$.

- Weak values and the Wigner transform (De Gosson, 2017, §12.3)
- Q-function Interpretation of Quantum Theory (Friederich, 2021; Schroeck, 2013).
- Kirkwood-Dirac Distribution (Umekawa, Lee, & Hatano, 2024).

7 Decoherence and Open Quantum Phase Space Mechanics

> Most interesting systems are much too complicated to be describable in practice by the underlying microscopic laws of physics. [...] Practical considerations force one to seek for a simpler, effectively probabilistic description in terms of an open system's dynamics. The use of probability theory allows the treatment of complex systems which involve a huge or even an infinite number of degrees of freedom. This is achieved by restricting the mathematical formulation to an appropriate set of a small number of relevant variables. Experience shows that under quite general physical conditions the time evolution of the relevant variables is governed by simple dynamical laws which can be formulated in terms of a set of effective equations of motion. The latter take into account the coupling to the remaining, irrelevant degrees of freedom in an approximate way through the inclusion of dissipative and stochastic terms.
>
> (Breuer & Petruccione, 2002, p.viii)

7.1 The Fourier Transform and the Heat Kernel

The long-standing and much remarked upon interplay between pure mathematics and applied physics has perhaps no more elegant illustration than the fact that the Fourier transform was invented as a means to solve the heat equation. Here we will briefly review some of the basic mathematics behind the Fourier transform solution to the heat equation with a view to the better understanding of the thermal basis of decoherence and open quantum phase space mechanics. For the most part we follow the elementary textbook discussion of Craig (2018).

Let us first introduce the notion of a *convolution operator*. Consider two integrable functions defined on the real line: $h(x), g(x) \in L^1(\mathbb{R}^1)$. The convolution operator is a product operation that returns a further function $(h*g)(x) \in L^1(\mathbb{R}^1)$ that is given by:

$$(h*g)(x) = \int_{-\infty}^{+\infty} h(x-x')f(x')dx' \qquad (7.1)$$

As such, we can think of the convolution of two functions as an integral product in which one function is reflected and shifted.

The convolution product is commutative and associative which means that if we have that $h(x), f(x), g(x) \in L^1(\mathbb{R}^1)$ then it is the case that:

$$(h * g)(x) = (g * h)(x) \tag{7.2}$$
$$(h * (g * f))(x) = ((h * g) * f)(x) \tag{7.3}$$

Furthermore, if we have that $\partial_x f \in L^1(\mathbb{R}^1)$ then we can show that the differentiation operation commutes with the operation of convolution:

$$\partial_x(h * f)(x) = h * (\partial_x f)(x) \tag{7.4}$$

Both these important properties of the convolution operator can be derived from the behaviour of the convolution operator under the Fourier transform.

Let us first define the *Fourier transform* of a function $g(x) \in L^1(\mathbb{R}^1)$ as

$$\mathcal{F}(g(x)) \equiv \hat{g}(\xi) = \frac{1}{\sqrt{2\pi}} \int_{-\infty}^{+\infty} e^{-i\xi x} g(x) dx \tag{7.5}$$

We will then also have that $\mathcal{F}(g(x)) \in L^1(\mathbb{R}^1)$. The inverse Fourier transform is then given by:

$$g(x) = \frac{1}{\sqrt{2\pi}} \int_{-\infty}^{+\infty} e^{-i\xi x} \hat{g}(\xi) d\xi \tag{7.6}$$

which we assume to be always well-defined. Further, it can be shown that $(\widehat{\partial_x f})(\xi) = i\xi \hat{f}(\xi)$ and thus that we can always re-express spatial derivatives in terms of the Fourier transform (Craig, 2018, Proposition 2.3).

Now, if we consider the Fourier transform of the convolution between $h(x), g(x) \in L^1(\mathbb{R}^1)$, we will have that $\mathcal{F}((h * g)(x))$ is given by:

$$\widehat{(h * g)}(\xi) = \int_{-\infty}^{+\infty} e^{i\xi x} \left(\int_{-\infty}^{+\infty} h(x - x') f(x') dx' \right) dx$$

$$= \frac{1}{\sqrt{2\pi}} \int_{-\infty}^{+\infty} \int_{-\infty}^{+\infty} e^{-i\xi(x-x')} h(x - x') e^{-i\xi x'} f(x') dx' dx$$

where we have used Fubini's theorem. This we can then re-write as:

$$= \sqrt{2\pi} \left(\frac{1}{\sqrt{2\pi}} \int_{-\infty}^{+\infty} e^{-i\xi x'} f(x') \left(\frac{1}{\sqrt{2\pi}} \int_{-\infty}^{+\infty} e^{-i\xi(x-x')} h(x - x') dx \right) dx' \right)$$
$$= \sqrt{2\pi} \hat{f}(\xi) \hat{h}(\xi)$$

We thus get the fundamental relation (sometimes called the *Convolution Theorem*) that *under Fourier transform convolution becomes multiplication*:

$$\widehat{h * g}(\xi) = \sqrt{2\pi} \hat{h}(\xi) \hat{g}(\xi) \tag{7.7}$$

From this it is straightforward to show that the convolution product is commutative and associative and commutes with differentiation as aforementioned.

Let us then consider the heat equation, which is a second-order homogenous partial differential equation of the form:

$$0 = (\partial_t - \frac{1}{2}\partial_x^2)u(t,x) \tag{7.8}$$

where $t \in \mathbb{R}_+^1$ and $x \in \mathbb{R}$.

Assume initial data $u(0,x) = f(x) \in L^1(\mathbb{R}^1)$ and that $u(t,x)$ is sufficiently well-behaved that we can define its Fourier inversion:

$$u(t,x) = \frac{1}{2\pi}\int_{-\infty}^{+\infty} e^{i\xi x}\hat{u}(t,\xi)d\xi \tag{7.9}$$

Using the relation $\widehat{(\partial_x f)}(\xi) = i\xi \hat{f}(\xi)$ which was assumed earlier we can re-write the heat equation as:

$$\frac{d}{dt}\hat{u}(t,\xi) = -\frac{1}{2}\xi^2\hat{u}(t,\xi) \tag{7.10}$$

which is a second-order ordinary differential equation with a solution of the form:

$$\hat{u}(t,\xi) = e^{-\frac{1}{2}\xi^2 t}\hat{u}(0,\xi) = e^{-\frac{1}{2}\xi^2 t}\hat{f}(\xi) \tag{7.11}$$

where $\hat{f}(\xi)$ is the Fourier transform of the initial data. We thus have the solution to the heat equation in Fourier transform space and simply need to transform back to get the solution in the original space.

$$u(t,x) = \frac{1}{2\pi}\int_{-\infty}^{+\infty} e^{i\xi x}\hat{u}(t,\xi)d\xi \tag{7.12}$$

$$= \frac{1}{2\pi}\int_{-\infty}^{+\infty} e^{i\xi x}(e^{-\frac{1}{2}\xi^2 t}\hat{f}(\xi))d\xi \tag{7.13}$$

$$= \frac{1}{2\pi}\int_{-\infty}^{+\infty}\int_{-\infty}^{+\infty} e^{i\xi(x-y)}e^{-\frac{1}{2}\xi^2 t}f(y)dyd\xi \tag{7.14}$$

$$= \int_{-\infty}^{+\infty}\frac{1}{2\pi}\left(\int_{-\infty}^{+\infty} e^{i\xi(x-y)}e^{-\frac{1}{2}\xi^2 t}d\xi\right)f(y)dy \tag{7.15}$$

$$= \int_{-\infty}^{+\infty} H(t,x-y)f(y)dy \tag{7.16}$$

where we have introduced the heat kernel function $H(t,x)$ which can be shown to have the explicit Gaussian form:

$$H(t,x) = \frac{1}{\sqrt{2\pi t}}e^{-\frac{1}{2}x^2/t} \tag{7.17}$$

The definition of the convolution product from earlier then allows us to write the general solution to the heat equation in terms of the convolution of the heat kernel with the initial data as:

$$u(t,x) = \int_{-\infty}^{+\infty} H(t, x-x') f(y) dx' \tag{7.18}$$

$$= (H(t, \cdot) * f)(x) \tag{7.19}$$

We thus arrive at the general result that the evolution equation for a smooth initial distribution under a diffusion equation (with constant diffusion coefficient) is equivalent to the convolution of the initial distribution with a Gaussian. This is the most physically important illustration of a *Weierstrass transform*, also known as Gaussian smoothing or Gaussian filter. The physical effect is for the initial distribution to be progressively smoothed towards a Gaussian distribution just as one would expect in a physical diffusion process. Such transformations have a fundamental importance in signal analysis and image processing. This physical understanding of the Weierstrass transform as Gaussian smoothing via heat kernel convolution will prove crucial to understanding decoherence in an open quantum phase space formalism.

7.2 Open and Closed Quantum Theory

In the context of quantum physics the distinction between closed and open is best understood as picking out the distinction between models that are unitary and non-unitary rather than between quantum systems that do or do not have interactions with an external environment. This way of understanding the open/closed distinctions accords with much but not all physical practice and is defended at length in Ladyman and Thebault (2024), which we partially follow in the following.

Let us first consider some important formal properties of unitarity in relation to probability, purity and entropy. First, most straightforwardly, unitarity is sufficient but not necessary for probability conservation since there are non-unitary dynamical equations that preserve probability. In particular, in the density matrix formalism, where a state is represented by a positive semi-definite operator of unit trace, ρ, a map is probability preserving if it is trace-preserving. A map being unitary then a sufficient but not necessary condition for a map to be trace-preserving.

In general, unitary time evolution conserves the *norm* induced by the inner product on Hilbert space. It can be shown that unitary time evolution is sufficient (although again not necessary) for the preservation of the *purity* of a quantum state when represented as a density operator. Explicitly, the purity of a state is given by $\gamma = \text{Tr}(\rho^2)$. Pure states are such that $\gamma = 1$. The quantum operation $\Lambda(\rho) = U\rho U^\dagger$ preserves the purity of ρ *if* U is a unitary operator (Jaeger, 2007).

Purity preservation is equivalent to the conservation of linear entropy since $S_L = 1 - \gamma$. There is also a connection between unitarity and the conservation of the informational or von Neumann entropy $S = -\text{Tr}(\rho \ln \rho)$. In particular, the von Neumann entropy is also invariant with respect to the quantum operation $\Lambda(\rho) = U\rho U^\dagger$ since we have that $S(U\rho U^\dagger) = S(\rho)$ (Breuer & Petruccione, 2002, §2.3). Hence, unitary closed system dynamics conserves both the linear and von Neumann entropies and non-unitary open system dynamics allows for entropy non-conservation.

To provide a concrete representation of open and closed system quantum models let us first consider the paradigmatic equation for a unitary quantum dynamics of density operators, the von Neumann equation:

$$\dot{\rho} = -i[H, \rho] \tag{7.20}$$

where the evolution of density operator ρ will be unitary provided the Hamiltonian H is self-adjoint. The von Neumann is simply the Schrödinger equation expressed in terms of the density matrix rather than the wavefunction.

The paradigmatic equation for open quantum systems is the Lindblad equation. The Lindblad equation is made up of a unitary part identical to the von Neumann equation together with a non-unitary part. For an initial pure state the unitary part reduces to the Schrödinger equation (hence, the Lindblad equation may be regarded as more general). In physical models the non-unitary part of the dynamics, encoded in a super-operator $\mathcal{D}(\rho)$, corresponds to a dissipator term that encodes the parameterised effects of decoherence, thermal damping and noise.

Explicitly, the Lindblad equation can be written:

$$\dot{\rho} = -i[H, \rho] + \sum_{i,j} a_{ij}(F_i \rho F_j^\dagger - \frac{1}{2}\{F_j^\dagger F_i, \rho\}) \tag{7.21}$$

$$= -i[H, \rho] + \mathcal{D}(\rho) \tag{7.22}$$

where the F_i are bounded operators, $\{,\}$ is the anti-commutator, and the matrix a_{ij} is positive semi-definite (Breuer & Petruccione, 2002, Eq. 3.63).

The more customary diagonal form of the equation is then given by re-writing the dissipator as (Breuer & Petruccione, 2002, Eq. 3.61):

$$\mathcal{D}(\rho) = \sum_{k=1}^{k=N^2-1} \gamma_k(A_k \rho A_k^\dagger - \frac{1}{2}A_k^\dagger A_k \rho - \frac{1}{2}\rho A_k^\dagger A_k) \tag{7.23}$$

$$= \sum_{k=1}^{k=N^2-1} \gamma_k([A_k \rho, A_k^\dagger] + [A_k, \rho A_k^\dagger]) \tag{7.24}$$

where

$$F_i = \sum_{k=1}^{k=N^2-1} u_{ki} A_k \tag{7.25}$$

and the u are unitaries such that the matrix $uau^\dagger$ is diagonal with non-negative eigenvalues γ_i.

The non-unitary dynamics of a system having the Lindblad form is a sufficient (but not necessary) condition for probability to be conserved. We can see this as follows, following Cuffaro and Hartmann (2024):

First, take the trace of both sides of the full Lindblad equation to arrive at:

$$\text{Tr}(\dot{\rho}(t)) = -\text{Tr}(i[H, \rho(t)]) + \text{Tr}(\mathcal{D}(\rho(t))) \tag{7.26}$$

The form of $\mathcal{D}(\rho(t))$ is given by (7.24). Then, since, in general, the trace of a commutator is always zero we then have that $\text{Tr}(\dot{\rho}(t)) = 0$. This then implies that $\frac{d}{dt}\text{Tr}(\rho(t)) = 0$ and thus that $\text{Tr}(\rho(0)) = \text{Tr}(\rho(t)) = 1$. Next, consider a complete set of measurements with outcomes m and corresponding projective operators M_m. We would then have that $\sum_m M_m^\dagger M_m = I$. Finally, if $p_m(t)$ is the probability of obtaining a measurement m then:

$$\sum_m p_m(t) = \sum_m \text{Tr}(\rho(t) M_m^\dagger M_m) \tag{7.27}$$

$$= \text{Tr} \sum_m (\rho(t) M_m^\dagger M_m) \tag{7.28}$$

$$= \text{Tr}(\rho(0)) = \text{Tr}(\rho(t)) = 1 \tag{7.29}$$

Hence $\sum_m p_m(t) = \sum_m p_m(0) = 1$.

We thus have that at the level of probability, open quantum dynamics should be expected to be globally probability conserving so long as it is modelled via a master equation in Lindblad form. This is entirely in keeping with our considerations of local quasi-probability fluid non-conservation that obtains in the case the Wigner-Moyal representation, even for closed quantum systems, since that formalism also shows both local conservation of probability for the marginals and global conservation of quasi-probability. Moreover, as shall be expounded in more detail in Section 8, the fact that open quantum system dynamics conserves the total probability of the state of the system encodes an important form of *modal autonomy* within the relevant models. The models can represent the evolution of possibilities of the open system consistently without reference to a further system despite the model being open. We will return to this idea later.

There is a natural connection between open quantum systems and classical contact systems. In particular, the semi-classical limit of an open quantum system model is typically a dissipative classical model as is indicated by the interpretation of the non-unitary part of the Lindblad equation as a dissipator. Most vividly, we can show that the Caldeira-Leggett master equation recovers the equations of motion for a damped Brownian particle when the Ehrenfest-type relations are used to derive the equations of motion for the first and second order moments. We will show this explicitly in the following section for the harmonic oscillator recovering the results of (Breuer & Petruccione, 2002, p. 175) but via the Wigner-Moyal formalism.

7.3 Semi-Classical Damped Quantum Oscillator

The Caldeira-Leggett equation (Breuer & Petruccione, 2002; Caldeira & Leggett, 1983) is an important example of a quantum master equation derived via the so-called system-reservoir approach. The derivation starts by considering a single particle moving in a potential as the system and then coupling the particle to a bath of harmonic oscillators. One then quantises the model, traces out the bath and applies a series of approximations leading to an open systems master equation for the quantum particle only that takes the characteristic form:

$$\frac{d\hat{\rho}}{dt} = -i[\hat{H},\hat{\rho}] - 2m\gamma k_B T[\hat{q},[\hat{q},\hat{\rho}]] - i\gamma[\hat{q},\{\hat{p},\hat{\rho}\}] \qquad (7.30)$$

where T is temperature, $\{,\}$ is the anti-commutator and we have assumed $\hbar = 1$. The equation is an open quantum model that can be derived from a closed quantum model of a particle coupled to a bath of oscillators. The density matrix is a reduced density matrix for the system after a suitable tracing operation and application of limits. For more details on the derivation see (Breuer & Petruccione, 2002, §3.6).

The first term in the Caldeira-Leggett equation is simply the normal unitary time evolution equation. The second term with the double commutator encodes the effects of decoherence. The third term then can be understood to encode the effects of dissipation at a quantum level. We will consider the significance of the second term in the following section. For the time being, let us focus our attention on the first and third terms only since these are the terms that feature in the Ehrenfest relation. This will allow us to explicitly demonstrate the connection to classical models of dissipation via the Wigner-Moyal formalism.

Let us start by multiplying out the anti-commutator and writing out the Caldeira-Leggett equation without the decoherence term (since this would drop out in the Ehrenfest relations in any case). From (7.30) we have:

$$\frac{d}{dt}\hat{\rho} = -\frac{i}{\hbar}\left([\hat{H},\hat{\rho}] + \gamma[\hat{q},\hat{p}\hat{\rho}] + \gamma[\hat{q},\hat{\rho}\hat{p}]\right) \qquad (7.31)$$

Applying (6.15) and (6.18) allows us to re-write the same master equation in the Wigner-Moyal formalism:

$$\frac{d}{dt}W = -\frac{i}{\hbar}(H \star W - W \star H)$$
$$- \frac{i\gamma}{\hbar}(q \star (p \star W) - (p \star W) \star q) \qquad (7.32)$$
$$- \frac{i\gamma}{\hbar}(q \star (W \star p) - (W \star p) \star q)$$

If we assume that $H = p^2 + q^2$ and apply the bidifferential operator representation of the Moyal star we get:

$$\frac{d}{dt}W = -\frac{i}{\hbar}\left[\left(q + \frac{i\hbar}{2}\overrightarrow{\partial_p}\right)^2 W - W\left(q - \frac{i\hbar}{2}\overleftarrow{\partial_p}\right)^2\right]$$
$$- \frac{i}{\hbar}\left[\left(p - \frac{i\hbar}{2}\overrightarrow{\partial_q}\right)^2 W - W\left(p + \frac{i\hbar}{2}\overleftarrow{\partial_q}\right)^2\right]$$
$$- \frac{i}{\hbar}\left[\left(q + \frac{i\hbar}{2}\overrightarrow{\partial_p}\right)\left(\left(p - \frac{i\hbar}{2}\overrightarrow{\partial_q}\right)W\right) - \left(\left(p - \frac{i\hbar}{2}\overrightarrow{\partial_q}\right)W\right)\left(q - \frac{i\hbar}{2}\overleftarrow{\partial_p}\right)\right]$$
$$- \frac{i}{\hbar}\left[\left(q + \frac{i\hbar}{2}\overrightarrow{\partial_p}\right)\left(W\left(p + \frac{i\hbar}{2}\overleftarrow{\partial_q}\right)\right) - \left(W\left(p + \frac{i\hbar}{2}\overleftarrow{\partial_q}\right)\right)\left(q - \frac{i\hbar}{2}\overleftarrow{\partial_p}\right)\right]$$
$$\frac{d}{dt}W = -p\frac{\partial W}{\partial q} + q\frac{\partial W}{\partial p}$$
$$- \frac{i}{\hbar}\left[\left(q + \frac{i\hbar}{2}\overrightarrow{\partial_p}\right)\left(pW + \frac{i\hbar}{2}\frac{\partial W}{\partial q}\right) - \left(pW + \frac{i\hbar}{2}\frac{\partial W}{\partial q}\right)\left(q - \frac{i\hbar}{2}\overleftarrow{\partial_p}\right)\right]$$
$$- \frac{i}{\hbar}\left[\left(q + \frac{i\hbar}{2}\overrightarrow{\partial_p}\right)\left(pW - \frac{i\hbar}{2}\frac{\partial W}{\partial q}\right) - \left(pW - \frac{i\hbar}{2}\frac{\partial W}{\partial q}\right)\left(q - \frac{i\hbar}{2}\overleftarrow{\partial_p}\right)\right]$$

Together these imply that the Caldeira-Leggett equation without the decoherence term is equivalent to a Fokker-Planck equation for the Wigner function of the form:

$$\frac{d}{dt}W = -p\frac{\partial W}{\partial q} + q\frac{\partial W}{\partial p} + 2\frac{\partial}{\partial p}(pW) \qquad (7.33)$$

The difference between the two entirely encoded in the difference between a Wigner quasi-probability distribution and a classical probability distribution as per our earlier discussions, that is, negativity, failure of localisability, and failure of local conservation over time.

The rate of change of the average of a time-independent quantum phase space function is then given by the analogue of (6.35) which is:

$$\frac{d\langle O \rangle}{dt} = \int dqdp \frac{\partial W}{\partial t} O \qquad (7.34)$$
$$= \frac{1}{i\hbar} \int dqdp\, [(H \star W - W \star H) \star O]$$

$$+ \gamma (q \star (p \star W) - (p \star W) \star q) \star O \qquad (7.35)$$
$$+ \gamma (q \star (W \star p) - (W \star p) \star q) \star O$$

We can then substitute in the Moyal brackets and use the triple product rule $A \star (B \star C) = (A \star B) \star C$ to re-write this as:

$$\frac{d\langle O \rangle}{dt} = \frac{1}{i\hbar} \int dq dp W[[A, H]]$$
$$+ \frac{\gamma}{i\hbar} \int dq dp \, [(p \star W)[[O, q]] + (W \star K)[[O, q]]]$$
$$= \langle [[O, H]] \rangle + \frac{\gamma}{i\hbar} \int dq dp \, [(p \star W)[[O, q]] + (W \star p)[[O, q]]]$$

Since $[[q, q]] = 0$ we immediately have that for $O = q$:

$$\frac{d\langle q \rangle}{dt} = \langle [[q, H]] \rangle \qquad (7.36)$$

which is identical to the closed quantum system expression (6.35). The familiar simple harmonic Hamiltonian, $H(q,p) = \frac{1}{2m}p^2 + \frac{1}{2}kq^2$, gives the explicit expression:

$$\frac{d\langle q \rangle}{dt} = \frac{1}{m}\langle p \rangle \qquad (7.37)$$

as per the free particle case consider in (6.54). More interestingly for $O = p$ we have that:

$$\frac{d\langle p \rangle}{dt} = \langle [[p, H]] \rangle + \frac{\gamma}{i\hbar} \int dq dp \, [(p \star W)[[p, q]] + (W \star p)[[p, q]]]$$
$$= \langle [[p, H]] \rangle + 2\gamma \int dq dp W K$$
$$= \langle [[p, H]] \rangle + 2\gamma \langle p \rangle$$

where we have assumed that $[[q, p]] = i\hbar$ and used (6.24). For the general Hamiltonian $H = \frac{1}{2m}p^2 + V(q)$ this will give us an expression that takes the form:

$$\frac{d\langle p \rangle}{dt} = \langle [[p, H]] \rangle + 2\gamma \langle p \rangle$$
$$= \langle [[p, V(q)]] \rangle + 2\gamma \langle p \rangle$$
$$= -\left\langle \frac{dV(q)}{dq} \right\rangle + 2\gamma \langle p \rangle$$

Where we have applied (6.41) once more. We thus have that $\langle q \rangle$ is given by the solution to the ODE:

$$\frac{d^2}{dt^2}\langle q \rangle + 2\gamma \frac{d}{dt}\langle q \rangle + 2\langle q \rangle = 0 \qquad (7.38)$$

which is of equation for a damped oscillator as expected.

We thus have a direct formal connection between classical contact systems and open quantum systems with dissipation. This could have been expected from the form of the equations for the first moments which is structurally very similar to the contact Hamilton's equations. Exploration of these connections is an outstanding and highly important physical and mathematical challenge. For recent work see Cruz-Prado, Bravetti, and Garcia-Chung (2021).

7.4 Wigner Negativity and Decoherence

Let us now consider the behaviour of the Wigner function within a simple model of decoherence with a focus on the role of Wigner negativity due to Joos and Zeh (1985). The Joos-Zeh equation can be derived based on a idealised decoherence model with recoilless scattering that carries away information but not momentum of a quantum particle. As such it is a minimal model for position localisation of a quantum particle via the destruction of coherence. More realistic models include noise and dissipation terms but share the central formal feature of Gaussian-smoothing via heat kernel convolution as per our earlier discussion.

The Joos-Zeh master equation takes the explicit form:

$$\frac{d\hat{\rho}}{dt} = -\frac{i}{2m}[\hat{p}^2, \hat{\rho}] - \frac{D}{2}[\hat{q},[\hat{q},\hat{\rho}]] \tag{7.39}$$

where we have assumed a free particle Hamiltonian and the decoherence time scale will be $t_0 = \sqrt{m/D}$. Physically, the localisation rate, D, measures how fast interference between different positions disappears for distances smaller than the wavelength of the scattered particles. It has units $cm^{-2}\ s^{-1}$ and includes a factor of $\hbar^{-2}$ and a linear dependence on temperature (Joos et al., 2013, §3.2.1). This is, of course, just the first two terms of the Caldeira-Leggett equation.

Using the same approach as before, the quantum phase space equation corresponding to (7.39) is given by a Fokker-Planck type-equation for the Wigner function:

$$\frac{\partial W}{\partial t} = -\frac{p}{m}\frac{\partial W}{\partial q} + \frac{D}{2}\frac{\partial^2 W}{\partial p^2} \tag{7.40}$$

As with the equation (7.33) we considered earlier, the expression has the same functional form as a Fokker-Planck type equation for a classical probability density function. However it is not physically equivalent to such an equation precisely because the Wigner function is a quasi-probability density with non-classical features (negativity, failure of localisability, and failure of local conservation) as per our earlier discussions.

Following Diósi and Kiefer (2002), the Fokker-Plank equation for the Wigner function can be demonstrated to be equivalent to a progressive

Gaussian-smoothing of an initial Wigner function $W(\Gamma; 0)$. In particular, we can re-write the Equation (7.40) as a convolution of the form:

$$W(\Gamma; t) = g(\Gamma; \mathbf{C}_W(t)) * W(x - pt/m, p; 0) \qquad (7.41)$$

where $g(\Gamma; \mathbf{C}_W(t))$ is a generalised Gaussian function with time-dependent correlation matrix:

$$\mathbf{C}_W(t) = Dt \begin{pmatrix} t^2/3m^2 & t/2m \\ t/2m & 1 \end{pmatrix} \qquad (7.42)$$

and we have used the $*$ symbol for the convolution operation to avoid confusion with the Moyal star product.

Convolution with a Gaussian function, as per the heat equation discussed earlier, has the general effect of smoothing the Wigner function. Furthermore, we can understand decoherence in terms of convolution of the Wigner function with a Gaussian according to a Weierstrass transform. This is, in fact, precisely to transform a Wigner function into a Husimi Q-function (Curtright et al., 2013, §13). As such, we should not expect the quantum mechanical marginal probabilities to be fully recoverable post-decoherence, which is perhaps unsurprising.

The regions of Wigner negativity are of order $\hbar$ and a Gaussian smoothing can be shown to be such that it will progressively render any initial Wigner function positive definite.[10] Indeed, Diósi and Kiefer (2002) show that by Equation (7.41), *any* initial state will be such that Wigner function will be strictly positive after a finite time t_D which is of the order of the decoherence timescale t_0 defined earlier. The result of Diósi and Kiefer (2002) demonstrates that even for the most simple model of decoherence the dynamical equations serve to smooth-out structure of the Wigner function and eliminate Wigner negativity almost immediately.

7.5 Further Topics of Study

- Decoherent Histories and Quasi-Measure Theory (Dowker & Wilkes, 2022; Sorkin, 1994).
- Semi-classical Limit of the Wigner Function (Berry, 1977; Mariño, 2021).
- Decoherence, the Semi-classicality limit, and Probability (Hernández, Ranard, & Riedel, 2023; Layton & Oppenheim, 2023).
- Wigner Positivity Without a von Neumann Term (Brody, Graefe, & Melanathuru, 2024).

---

[10] This is true for Gaussian smoothings but does not hold in general for any averaging (de Aguiar & de Almeida, 1990).

8 Representation and Possibility

This final section will knit together some of the key ideas of the foregoing six in the context of our unifying philosophical themes. Our initial focus will be upon the philosophical significance of phase space formulations of classical and quantum mechanical theories understood as possibility space representations with particular reference to the role of Liouville theorem and its failure for the analysis of the *representational capacities* of such spaces. We will then turn to analysis of the modal structure of phase spaces and the idea of appealing to a form of modal expressivism to both avoid the placement problem for such structure and better to understanding its pragmatic function.

8.1 Classical Possibility Space Representations

The choice of a symplectic manifold as the representational space for the states of a family of physical systems has significant implications for the relations between physical possibilities that our possibility space has the capacity to represent. Most straightforwardly, symplectic manifolds come equipped with a standard of isomorphism, symplectomorphism, and as such we can immediately apply the norm of Weatherall (2018) and assert that since isomorphic mathematical models in physics *should* be taken to have the same representational capacities, if a particular symplectic manifold may be used to represent a given structured set of possible states of affairs, then any symplectomorphic model be used to represent that a given structured set of possible states of affairs equally well. In physical practice, this crucial feature of symplectic manifolds corresponds to our ability to choose arbitrary canonical charts on phase space. Although the representational norm is implicit in physical and mathematical practice it is worth stating explicitly at least to clarify that the canonical momentum variables only correspond to Newtonian momentum in a preferred chart, *pace* Chua and Callender (2021).

The geometric structure of a symplectic manifold provides us with a framework for representing physical systems as Hamiltonian systems. Hamiltonian systems represent dynamical possible models of a theory as flows generated by Hamilton vector fields. These flows are constrained to preserve the symplectic structure that encodes the relationship between the instantaneous position and canonical momenta variables. This, in turn, implies through Liouville's theorem that the phase space volume the trajectories cut-out occupy a constant volume of phase space over time. Thus, for any Hamiltonian system, a given family of dynamically possible models will occupy a constant *volume of possibility space* over time.

In the formal mode, Liouville's theorem is a well-known feature of phase space representations. The interpretative implications of the theorem do not, however, seem to have been subject to any previous philosophical discussion. In particular, the theorem constrains the capacity of the space to represent only sets of possibilities that maintain their distinct evolutions. Since phase space volume is conserved, every set of instantaneous possibilities picked out by a dynamical curve will remain distinct. In general, phase spaces with symplectic structure, and thus a Liouville theorem, cannot represent (fine-grained) sets of possibilities which have 'attractors' such that there is a particular possibility that gets preferentially selected towards over time.

In the context of a stochastic phase space representations, Liouville's theorem implies that the probability flow is 'incompressible'. This has similar but non-identical implications for the relations between possibilities that a stochastic possibility space has the capacity to represent. That is, like in the Hamiltonian case, Liouville's theorem constrains the capacity of the space to represent only sets of possibilities that maintain their distinct evolutions. However, a stochastic possibility space has more structure and thus more representational capacity: the constraint embodies in Liouville's theorem is manifested in terms of both in the preservation of the underlying unit volume and in the incompressibility the flow of the probability density fluid.

The choice of a symplectic manifold as the representational space for the states of a family of physical systems is also *restrictive* with regard to relations between possibilities that our possibility space has the capacity to represent. In particular, the geometric structure of Hamiltonian systems and symplectic manifolds is such that we *cannot* represent families of physical systems endowed with modal structure corresponding to the shrinking of volumes of possibility space over time. In the stochastic case this, of course, corresponds to the fact that the space cannot represent compression (or expansion) of probability fluid flow and thus the existence of sinks and sources of probability current.

The contrast we have in mind here is with contact manifolds. Such spaces can be used to represent structured sets of possibilities in which Liouville's theorem is violated and there is compression (or expansion) of the local volume form on contact phase space. This can be understood as a local compression (or expansion) of *solutions* along surfaces transverse to the dynamical flow. One can then represent sets of possibilities that do not maintain their distinct evolutions. Since contact phase space volume is not conserved sets of instantaneous possibilities picked out by a dynamical curves will not necessarily remain distinct.

In general, phase spaces with contact structure, and thus violation of Liouville's theorem, can represent (fine-grained) sets of possibilities which have 'attractors' such that there is a particular possibility that gets preferentially selected towards over time.

Consider a set of damped oscillators with family members corresponding to different initial velocity and momentum. Over time we expect the volume of possibility space occupied by the family to approach zero since, due to the damping, the dynamics will eventually lead all the oscillators to a single possible state of a stationary oscillator at the zero potential position. The space thus has the capacity to represent modal structure in which we have convergence between possible histories of the world in which the same physical system but different initial conditions are instantiated. This rich representational structure also, of course, allows the representation of measure expansion and thus modal structure in which the volume of possibility space taken up by a set of possible states expands rather than contracts. Although physically difficult to conceptualise such behaviour is just the time reverse of the convergence behaviour. As such, plausibly the capacity to represent it corresponds to the ability of a contact manifold to represent worlds with a reversed (local) arrow of time.

The failure of Liouville's theorem is the context of contact phase space mechanics thus encodes a representational capacity for modal structures that goes beyond that of symplectic phase space mechanics. We should, however, note the strong formal similarities between the two spaces, notwithstanding the crucial formal differences. In particular, just as contact structure induces contact Hamiltonian vector fields in analogy to how symplectic structure induces (symplectic) Hamiltonian vector fields, we can identify a general class of structure perservering maps on a contact manifold that are the analogue of symplectomorphisms. These are contactomophisms.

Applying the norm of Weatherall (2018) once more, we can assert that since isomorphic mathematical models in physics should be taken to have the same representational capacities, if a particular contact manifold may be used to represent a given structured set of possible states of affairs, then any contactomophic model be used to represent that structured set of possible states of affairs equally well. The interconnections between contact and symplectic manifolds can be pushed even further once we recognise that in many (if not all) physical contexts it is possible to map between contact and symplectic representations of the same underlying physical degrees of freedom (Bravetti et al., 2020). The implications of such procedures for the representational structure of possibility spaces warrants considerable further study.

8.2 Quantum Possibility Space Representations

Let us now turn to quantum phase space mechanics and consider some attendant questions relating to representation and possibility. In this context it proves highly instructive to distinguish the specific way in which Liouville's theorem fails in the context of contact phase space mechanics from form of failure found in quantum phase space mechanics. In particular, we can contrast the non-Liouville representational capacity of a contact Hamiltonian phase space with that of a quantum phase space. Liouville's theorem fails but this failure is not dependent upon the underlying phase space geometry, but rather upon the further structures that were placed upon the space. In particular, the non-commutative Moyal-bracket structure of quantum phase space leads to a representation in which the quasi-probability function displays a 'fluid' flow that is no longer incompressible and shows local failure of conservation about a point. Over the entire phase space, however, the quasi-probability density is conserved. We thus have the capacity to represent quantum dynamics in which the total probability – trace of the density matrix – is conserved.

The particular local failure of Liouville's theorem is one of the features of quantum phase space representations that allows them to encode characteristic non-classical aspects of quantum systems. Another feature is the inability of quantum phase space representations to admit quasi-probability densities which are localised of order $\hbar$. The contrast here is with classical stochastic phase space representations where the Dirac delta function is an admissible probability density function. The respective difference in representational capacity is with regard to whether the two spaces can represent states of affairs that are determinate in position and momentum. Classical stochastic phase space representations do not encode Heisenberg uncertainty structure and are thus able to represent states of affairs that are determinate in position and momentum. Quantum phase space representations do encode Heisenberg uncertainty structure and are thus not able to represent states of affairs that are determinate in position and momentum at order $\hbar$. This feature is formally connected to the bound on the Wigner function.

The final core feature of quantum phase space representations that allows them to encode characteristic non-classical aspects of quantum systems is Wigner negativity. That the quasi-probability densities are valued on the negative part of the real line of course indicates a deep conceptual difference between these functions and classical probability functions. Indeed, this feature is connected to the phase space representation of non-classical properties such as entanglement and contextuality. The patches of negativity are of size order $\hbar$, and thus, the quantum phase space formalism includes a dimensionfull representation of the *size* of non-classical behaviour.

Open quantum system phase space representations all us to represent quantum systems interacting with an environment. In the most general sense such representations are under-constrained. In particular, if we consider the most general possible master equation then we find the possibility space structure that can be represented includes not just non-unitary dynamics and dissipation but also global failure of probability conservation. If, however, we restrict to maps which preserve the trace then we will recover global probability conservation.

The Lindblad form of quantum master equations provide a general framework for representing probability conserving systems since they have a dynamical structure that encodes a sufficient condition for the preservation of total probability. A quantum phase space with Lindblad dynamics thus has the capacity to represent states of affairs in which probability is conserved, but coherence is lost. What is more it can represent such states of affairs in an autonomous way (Ladyman & Thebault, 2024). The fact that open quantum system dynamics conserves the total probability of the state of the system encodes an important form of *modal autonomy* within the relevant models. The models can represent the evolution of possibilities of the open system consistently without reference to a further system despite the model being open in the sense of representing dynamics in which coherence is lost.

In the phase space representation, loss of coherence is represented in terms of the suppression of negativity of the Wigner quasi-probability function. This can be studied explicitly in terms of the Joos-Zeh model in which we can understand suppression of negativity in terms of a Gaussian-smoothing of the Wigner function. Since Wigner negativity encodes characteristic non-classical features within a quantum phase space representation, the smoothing of a quasi-probability function then represents successive removal of one key quantum feature of phase space representations via a diachronic dynamical process. It is worth remaking that in the context of more general classes of master equations key *qualitative* feature encoded in quantum phase representations has been applied in the context of analysis of the emergence of classical chaos from quantum systems (Franklin, 2023; Habib, Shizume, & Zurek, 1998).

The Caldeira-Leggett equation is an open system model which combines the decoherence term of the Joos-Zeh model with a further dissipation term. The model has the capacity to represent states of affairs that share the characteristic structure of contact systems when considered in the semi-classical Ehrenfest limit. In particular, we find that the form of the Ehrenfest equations for the Caldeira-Leggett master equation partially isomorphic to the contact Hamilton's equations. A quantum phase space representation with a master equation of the Caldeira-Leggett form thus has the capacity to represent, for example, the stochastic damped classical oscillator via the dynamics of its first moments.

Classical and quantum phase spaces have distinct representational capacities as encoded in the structure of the underlying geometric space and further algebraic, probability and quasi-probability structures placed upon them. Such *modal structures* allows us to express *characteristic features* of structured sets of physical possibilities. With this in mind let us return to the problem of understanding the *novel function* modal structure of possibility spaces within our scientific and philosophical vocabulary.

8.3 A Modal Revolution

Recall from Section 1.2 that following Price and Brandom we introduced the idea of *modal expressivism* as a response to the placement problem for modal structure. The idea is to follow the standard expressivist line in responding to the problem of situating a particular class of things that feature in our vocabulary without expanding our ontology. We assert that modal language is not in the business of 'describing reality' and offer some other positive account of what functional role this language plays in our linguistic lives. Rather, we understand modal structural vocabulary within possibility space representations as being as being pragmatic dependent on descriptive vocabulary in that modal vocabulary can be elaborated from the use of descriptive vocabulary.

We also considered the idea, contra Brandom, that the *novel modal vocabulary* of possibility space representations equips us with new ways of expanding our empirical descriptive vocabulary. Modal vocabulary still has a pragmatic dependence on descriptive vocabulary, in this case the descriptions of states of the world encoded in points in possibility spaces, but it can do much more than simply make explicit already acquired functions of that vocabulary. It can equipped us with new expressive tools. An alternative interpretation, more in keeping with Brandom's approach, would to frame the novelty of the relevant modal concepts as being only respect to the natural vs. scientific languages rather than the empirical descriptive vocabulary *per se*. On this more approach, it is descriptive features of *scientific language*, not contained in ordinary descriptive language, that are made explicit via the modal structure of phase space. The challenge to such an account is to provide a detailed meta-semantic account of how the process of 'making explicit' functions in the scientific context. In particular, how scientific modal concepts might be explicated from a descriptive vocabulary that lacks, for example, the inherently modal concept of phase space structure. In either case, there is an interesting and potentially highly productive project of fleshing out the meta-semantic details of a modal expressivist account of phase space structure.

In the context of the content of the previous six sections the basic strategy of modal expressivism ideas can be further explicated as follows. Modal expressivism lets us interpret phase space representations such that the modal structure (such as that encoded in Liouville's theorem) does not itself stand in a representation relation. Rather, it encodes normatively significant, robust counterfactual relations among empirical phenomena (such as stable dynamical relations between possibilities) in virtue of which phase space descriptions do not merely label, but discriminate and classify states of affairs. That is, phase space representations are able to articulate *inference-worthy* relationships among empirical possibilities such as conservative or dissipative behaviour or localisability or its failure.

There is then a normativitity of modal structure that comes from its role determining what counts as a good *explanatory* inference, and more generally *qualitative* inference, about physical phenomena that does not depend upon considering specific trajectories of states in phase space. In this way, we can understand the revolutionary transition towards qualitative mechanics as initiated by Poincaré, as a fundamentally *modal revolution*. By providing us with new methods to study the structure of possibility space, phase space mechanics allows us to equip our descriptive vocabulary with new uses and, moreover, enlarges the range of our inductive inferences regarding physical phenomena greatly beyond what is possible within a purely quantitive approach. Mechanics is modal structure in phase space.

References

Abraham, R., & Marsden, J. E. (1980). *Foundations of mechanics* (2nd ed.). American Mathematical Soc.

Adesso, G., Ragy, S., & Lee, A. R. (2014). Continuous variable quantum information: Gaussian states and beyond. *Open Systems & Information Dynamics*, *21*(01n02), 1440001.

Aniello, P. (2016). Functions of positive type on phase space, between classical and quantum, and beyond. *Journal of Physics: Conference Series*, *670*, 012004.

Arageorgis, A., Earman, J., & Ruetsche, L. (2017). Additivity requirements in classical and quantum probability https://philsci-archive.pitt.edu/13024/.

Arnol'd, V. I. (2013). *Mathematical methods of classical mechanics* (Vol. 60). Springer Science & Business Media.

Arnold, V. I., & Givental, A. B. (2001). *Dynamical systems iv: Symplectic geometry and its applications* (Vol. 4). Springer Science & Business Media.

Arnold, V. I., Kozlov, V. V., & Neishtadt, A. I. (2006). *Mathematical aspects of classical and celestial mechanics*. Springer.

Baker, G. A. (1958). Formulation of quantum mechanics based on the quasi-probability distribution induced on phase space. *Physical Review*, *109*(6), 2198.

Ballentine, L., & McRae, S. (1998). Moment equations for probability distributions in classical and quantum mechanics. *Physical Review A*, *58*(3), 1799.

Ballentine, L., Yang, Y., & Zibin, Z. P. (1994). Inadequacy of Ehrenfest's theorem to characterize the classical regime. *Physical review A*, *50*(4), 2854.

Barnett, S., & Radmore, P. M. (2002). *Methods in theoretical quantum optics* (Vol. 15). Oxford University Press.

Barrett, T. W. (2019). Equivalent and inequivalent formulations of classical mechanics. *The British Journal for the Philosophy of Science 70*(4), 1167–1199.

Belot, G. (2007, January). The representation of time and change in mechanics. In J. Butterfield & J. Earman (eds.), *Handbook of philosophy of physics* (chap. 2). Elsevier 133–227.

Berenstain, N., & Ladyman, J. (2011). Ontic structural realism and modality. In *Structural realism: Structure, object, and causality* (pp. 149–168). Springer.

Berry, M. V. (1977). Semi-classical mechanics in phase space: a study of Wigner's function. *Philosophical Transactions of the Royal Society of London. Series A, Mathematical and Physical Sciences*, *287*(1343), 237–271.

Booth, R. I., Chabaud, U., & Emeriau, P.- E. (2022). Contextuality and Wigner negativity are equivalent for continuous-variable quantum measurements. *Physical Review Letters*, *129*(23), 230401.

Bradley, C. (2024a, August). Do first-class constraints generate gauge transformations? a geometric resolution. *https://philsci-archive.pitt.edu/23730/*.

Bradley, C. (2024b, August). The relationship between Lagrangian and Hamiltonian mechanics: The irregular case. *https://philsci-archive.pitt.edu/23799/*.

Brandom, R. B. (2015). *From empiricism to expressivism: Brandom reads sellars*. Harvard University Press.

Bravetti, A., Cruz, H., & Tapias, D. (2017). Contact Hamiltonian mechanics. *Annals of Physics*, *376*, 17–39.

Bravetti, A., de León, M., Marrero, J. C., & Padrón, E. (2020). Invariant measures for contact Hamiltonian systems: symplectic sandwiches with contact bread. *Journal of Physics A: Mathematical and Theoretical*, *53*(45), 455205.

Bravetti, A., Jackman, C., & Sloan, D. (2023). Scaling symmetries, contact reduction and Poincaré's dream. *Journal of Physics A: Mathematical and Theoretical*, *56*(43), 435203.

Bravetti, A., & Tapias, D. (2015). Liouville's theorem and the canonical measure for nonconservative systems from contact geometry. *Journal of Physics A: Mathematical and Theoretical*, *48*(24), 245001.

Breuer, H.- P., & Petruccione, F. (2002). *The theory of open quantum systems*. Oxford University Press.

Brody, D. C., Graefe, E.- M., & Melanathuru, R. (2024). Phase-space measurements, decoherence and classicality. *arXiv preprint arXiv:2406.19628*.

Butterfield, J. (2007). On symplectic reduction in classical mechanics. In J. Butterfield & J. Earman (eds.), *Philosophy of physics* (1–131). Elsevier.

Caldeira, A. O., & Leggett, A. J. (1983). Path integral approach to quantum Brownian motion. *Physica A: Statistical mechanics and its Applications*, *121*(3), 587–616.

Carnap, R. (1934). *Logische syntax der sprache*. Vienna: Springer.

Case, W. B. (2008). Wigner functions and Weyl transforms for pedestrians. *American Journal of Physics*, *76*(10), 937–946.

Chua, E. Y., & Callender, C. (2021). No time for time from no-time. *Philosophy of Science*, *88*(5), 1172–1184.

Cohen, L. (1966). Can quantum mechanics be formulated as a classical probability theory? *Philosophy of Science*, *33*(4), 317–322.

Craig, W. (2018). *A course on partial differential equations* (Vol. 197). American Mathematical Soc.

Cruz-Prado, H., Bravetti, A., & Garcia-Chung, A. (2021). From geometry to coherent dissipative dynamics in quantum mechanics. *Quantum Reports*, *3*(4), 664–683.

Cuffaro, M. E., & Hartmann, S. (2024). The open systems view. *Philosophy of Physics*, *2*(6), 1–27.

Curiel, E. (2014). Classical mechanics is Lagrangian; it is not Hamiltonian. *The British Journal for the Philosophy of Science*, 269–321.

Curtright, T. L., Fairlie, D. B., & Zachos, C. K. (2013). *A concise treatise on quantum mechanics in phase space*. World Scientific.

Daubechies, I. (1983). Continuity statements and counterintuitive examples in connection with Weyl quantization. *Journal of Mathematical Physics*, *24*(6), 1453–1461.

Dawid, R., & Thébault, K. P. (2025). Decoherence and probability. *Philosophy of Science*, 1–26 DOI: https://doi.org/10.1017/psa.2025.10110.

de Aguiar, M. A., & de Almeida, A. O. (1990). On the probability density interpretation of smoothed Wigner functions. *Journal of Physics A: Mathematical and General*, *23*(19), L1025.

De Gosson, M. A. (2017). *The Wigner transform*. World Scientific.

Delfosse, N., Okay, C., Bermejo-Vega, J., Browne, D. E., & Raussendorf, R. (2017). Equivalence between contextuality and negativity of the wigner function for qudits. *New Journal of Physics*, *19*(12), 123024.

Dell'Antonio, G. (2016). *Lectures on the mathematics of quantum mechanics ii: Selected topics*. Springer.

Dewar, N. (2022). *Structure and equivalence*. Cambridge University Press.

Dias, N. C., de Gosson, M. A., & Prata, J. N. (2019). A refinement of the Robertson–Schrödinger uncertainty principle and a Hirschman–Shannon inequality for Wigner distributions. *Journal of Fourier Analysis and Applications*, *25*(1), 210–241.

Diósi, L., & Kiefer, C. (2002). Exact positivity of the wigner and p-functions of a Markovian open system. *Journal of Physics A: Mathematical and General*, *35*(11), 2675.

Dowker, F., & Wilkes, H. (2022). An argument for strong positivity of the decoherence functional in the path integral approach to the foundations of quantum theory. *AVS Quantum Science*, *4*(1), 012601.

Dubois, J., Saalmann, U., & Rost, J. M. (2021). Semi-classical Lindblad master equation for spin dynamics. *Journal of Physics A: Mathematical and Theoretical*, *54*(23), 235201.

Dudley, R. M. (2010). *Real analysis and probability*. Cambridge University Press.

Feintzeig, B. H. (2022). *The classical–quantum correspondence*. Cambridge University Press.

Feller, W. (1991). *An introduction to probability theory and its applications, volume 2* (Vol. 81). John Wiley & Sons.

Fletcher, S. C. (2020). On representational capacities, with an application to general relativity. *Foundations of Physics*, *50*(4), 228–249.

Franklin, A. (2023). Incoherent? no, just decoherent: How quantum many worlds emerge. *Philosophy of Science*, https://doi.org/10.1017/psa.2023.155.

French, S. (2011). Metaphysical underdetermination: why worry? *Synthese*, *180*(2), 205–221.

Friederich, S. (2021). Introducing the q-based interpretation of quantum theory. *British Journal for the Philosophy of Science*, *75*(3), https://doi.org/10.1086/716196.

Gibbs, J. W. (1902). *Elementary principles in statistical mechanics: Developed with especial reference to the rational foundations of thermodynamics*. C. Scribner's Sons.

Goroff, D. L. (1993). Editor's introduction to new methods of celestial mechanics by Henri Poincaré. *American Institute of Physics*.

Gotay, M. J., & Isenberg, G. (1992). La symplectification de la science. *Gazette des Mathématiciens*, *54*, 59–79.

Gryb, S., & Thébault, K. P. Y. (2023). *Time regained: Symmetry and evolution in classical mechanics*. Oxford University Press.

Guff, T., & Rocco, A. (2023). Time-reversal symmetry in open classical and quantum systems. *arXiv preprint arXiv:2311.08486*.

Habib, S., Shizume, K., & Zurek, W. H. (1998). Decoherence, chaos, and the correspondence principle. *Physical Review Letters*, *80*, 4361–4365. https://doi.org/10.1103/PhysRevLett.80.4361.

Hernández, F., Ranard, D., & Riedel, C. J. (2023). The *hbar* to 0 limit of open quantum systems with general Lindbladians: vanishing noise ensures classicality beyond the Ehrenfest time. *arXiv preprint arXiv:2307.05326*.

Hillery, M., O'Connell, R. F., Scully, M. O., & Wigner, E. P. (1984). Distribution functions in physics: Fundamentals. *Physics Reports*, *106*(3), 121–167.

Holm, D. D. (2011). *Geometric mechanics-part i: Dynamics and symmetry*. World Scientific.

Hudson, R. L. (1974). When is the Wigner quasi-probability density nonnegative? *Reports on Mathematical Physics*, *6*(2), 249–252.

Huggett, N., Lizzi, F., & Menon, T. (2021). Missing the point in noncommutative geometry. *Synthese, 199*, 4695–4728.

Jaeger, G. (2007). *Quantum information*. Springer.

Joos, E., & Zeh, H. D. (1985). The emergence of classical properties through interaction with the environment. *Zeitschrift für Physik B Condensed Matter, 59*, 223–243.

Joos, E., Zeh, H. D., Kiefer, C. Giulini, D. J., Kupsch, J., & Stamatescu, I.-O. (2013). *Decoherence and the appearance of a classical world in quantum theory*. Springer Science & Business Media.

Kosmann-Schwarzbach, Y. (2010). *The Noether theorems: Invariance and conservation laws in the twentieth century*. Springer Science & Business Media.

Kostant, B. (1970). Quantization and unitary representations. In *Lectures in modern analysis and applications iii* (pp. 87–208). Springer.

Ladyman, J. (1998). What is structural realism? *Studies in History and Philosophy of Science Part A, 29*(3), 409–424.

Ladyman, J. (2023). Structural Realism. In E. N. Zalta & U. Nodelman (eds.), *The Stanford encyclopedia of philosophy* (Summer 2023 ed.). Metaphysics Research Lab, Stanford University. https://plato.stanford.edu/archives/sum2023/entries/structural-realism/.

Ladyman, J. (2024). Patterns all the way up: Prolegomena to a future naturalised metaphysics, https://philpapers.org/rec/LADPAT-4.

Ladyman, J., & Lorenzetti, L. (2023). Effective ontic structural realism. *British Journal for the Philosophy of Science* (https://doi.org/10.1086/729061).

Ladyman, J., & Ross, D. (2007). *Every thing must go: Metaphysics naturalized*. Oxford University Press.

Ladyman, J., & Thebault, K. P. (2024). Open systems and autonomy. *philsci-archive.pitt.edu/23701/*.

Landsman, N. P. (2012). *Mathematical topics between classical and quantum mechanics*. Springer Science & Business Media.

Layton, I., & Oppenheim, J. (2023). The classical-quantum limit. *arXiv preprint arXiv:2310.18271*.

Lee, J. M. (2003). *Smooth manifolds*. Springer.

Leith, C. (1996). Stochastic models of chaotic systems. *Physica D: Nonlinear Phenomena, 98*(2–4), 481–491.

Leonhardt, U. (2010). *Essential quantum optics: From quantum measurements to black holes*. Cambridge University Press.

Lieb, E. H., & Loss, M. (2001). *Analysis* (Vol. 14). American Mathematical Soc.

Lyon, A., & Colyvan, M. (2008). The explanatory power of phase spaces. *Philosophia mathematica*, *16*(2), 227–243.

Malament, D. B. (2012). *Topics in the foundations of general relativity and Newtonian gravitation theory*. University of Chicago Press.

Mariño, M. (2021). *Advanced topics in quantum mechanics*. Cambridge University Press.

Marsden, J. E. (1992). *Lectures on mechanics* (Vol. 174). Cambridge University Press.

Marsden, J. E., & Ratiu, T. S. (2013). *Introduction to mechanics and symmetry: a basic exposition of classical mechanical systems* (Vol. 17). Springer Science & Business Media.

North, J. (2009). The 'structure' of physics: A case study? *The Journal of Philosophy*, *106*, 57–88.

O'Connell, R., & Wigner, E. (1981). Quantum-mechanical distribution functions: Conditions for uniqueness. *Physics Letters A*, *83*(4) 145–148.

Olver, P. J. (2000). *Applications of lie groups to differential equations* (2nd ed., Vol. 107). Springer Science & Business Media.

Pathria, R., & Beale, P. (2011). *Statistical mechanics* (3rd ed.). Elsevier.

Post, H. R. (1971). Correspondence, invariance and heuristics: In praise of conservative induction. *Studies in History and Philosophy of Science Part A*, *2*(3), 213–255.

Price, H. (2008). Will there be blood? Brandom, Hume, and the genealogy of modals. *Philosophical Topics*, *36*(2), 87–97.

Rickles, D. (2007). *Symmetry, structure, and spacetime*. Elsevier.

Risken, H. (1996). *The fokker-planck equation.* Springer.

Roberts, B. W. (2022). *Reversing the arrow of time*. Cambridge University Press.

Saunders, S. (1993). To what physics corresponds. In S. French, & H. Kamminga (eds.), *Correspondence, invariance and heuristics: Essays in honour of Heinz Post* (pp. 295–325). Springer.

Schroeck, F. E. (2013). *Quantum mechanics on phase space* (Vol. 74). Springer Science & Business Media.

Sneed, J. D. (1970). Quantum mechanics and classical probability theory. *Synthese*, 21, 34–64.

Sorkin, R. D. (1994). Quantum mechanics as quantum measure theory. *Modern Physics Letters A*, *9*(33), 3119–3127.

Souriau, J.-M. (1974). Sur la variété de kepler. In *Symposia mathmatica* (Vol. 14, pp. 343-260). Academic Press.

Souriau, J.-M. (2012). *Structure of dynamical systems: A symplectic view of physics* (Vol. 149). Springer Science & Business Media.

Suppes, P. (1961). Probability concepts in quantum mechanics. *Philosophy of Science*, *28*(4), 378–389.

Thébault, K. P. (2016). Quantization as a guide to ontic structure. *The British Journal for the Philosophy of Science*, 67 (1), 89-114.

Thébault, K. P. Y. (2011, May). *Symplectic reduction and the problem of time in nonrelativistic mechanics.* http://philsci-archive.pitt.edu/8623/.

Umekawa, S., Lee, J., & Hatano, N. (2024). Advantages of the kirkwood–Dirac distribution among general quasi-probabilities on finite-state quantum systems. *Progress of Theoretical and Experimental Physics*, *2024*(2), 023A02.

Wallace, D. (2021). Probability and irreversibility in modern statistical mechanics: Classical and quantum. *arXiv preprint arXiv:2104.11223*.

Weatherall, J. O. (2018). Regarding the 'hole argument'. *The British Journal for the Philosophy of Science*, 69 (2), 329–350.

Weedbrook, C., Pirandola, S., García-Patrón, R. et al. (2012). Gaussian quantum information. *Reviews of Modern Physics*, *84*(2), 621.

Wigner, E. (1932). On the quantum correction for thermodynamic equilibrium. *Physical Review*, *40*(5), 749.

Wigner, E. (1979). Quantum-Mechanical Distribution Functions Revisited. In W. Yourgrau & A. van der Merwe (eds.), *Perspectives in quantum theory,* (p. 25). Dover.

Wigner, E. P. (1971). Quantum-mechanical distribution functions revisited. In *Part i: Physical chemistry. part ii: Solid state physics* (pp. 251–262). Springer.

Acknowledgements

My interest in the topics covered in this Element spans my academic career thus far. I was first introduced to symplectic geometry as an advanced undergraduate at the University of Oxford by Oliver Pooley. I have been fascinated by the foundational and philosophical implications of representing mechanical theories within this formalism since then. By contrast, my interest in the quantum phase space formalism is much more recent and is connected to a collaborative project I have undertaken with Richard Dawid from the University of Stockholm. These topics, together with the others discussed in this Element, have been at the forefront of my thoughts over the last two or three years in particular, and I fear that the list of individuals that I have variously pestered, bothered, bored, or in any other ways inconvenienced by my desire to discuss them at great length will inevitably be incomplete. What follows is my best account of recollection.

I have had highly productive conversations about quasi-probability representations in quantum theory with Alex Franklin from Kings College London, Tony Short from the University of Bristol, Simon Saunders from the University of Oxford, Simon Friederich, Mritunjay Tyagi and Sean Gryb from University College Groningen, Dieter Schuch at the Goethe University Frankfurt, Christian Röken from the University of Bonn, Dorje Brody at the University of Surrey, and Rishindra Melanathuru at Imperial College London. In wrestling with my own confusion about non-classical probability, I have had the great pleasure of listening to various talks and having numerous discussions with wonderful colleagues at the University of Bristol, Kevin Blackwell, Catrin Campbell-Moore, Richard Pettigrew, Jason Konek, Jer Steeger, and Arthur Van Camp.

What little I know about contact geometry has been inspired by conversations and collaborations with David Sloan from the University of Lancaster and Sean Gryb from the University College Groningen. My interest in open quantum systems has been inspired by the path-breaking work of Stephan Hartman and Mike Cuffaro and deepened via discussions with Sébastien Rivat, all at LMU Munich. I have profited hugely in my thinking about modal structure and autonomy in open and closed systems through the immense good fortune to have James Ladyman as a colleague at the University of Bristol. Much of the text has benefitted from discussions and collaborations with James. I am also hugely grateful to Tushar Menon at MIT for extensive discussions regarding modal expressivism which has retroactively become the central theme of this Element. I am also hugely grateful to Ben Feintzeig at the University of Washington and Cosmas Zachos at the Argonne National Laboratory for highly valuable email correspondence and to James Ladyman, Tushar Menon, Rupert Smith, and two anonymous referees for written comments on various stages of draft material.

I have been particularly lucky to work with Stephan, Mike, James, Sebastian and Dave together on the AHRC-DFG project "The Universe as an Open System" [Ref: AH/W010569/1(AHRC)/468374455 (DFG)]. Work on this Element was partially supported by that grant together with the John Templeton Foundation project "Life on the Edge: Quantum Thermodynamics, Quantum Biology and the Arrow of Time" [grant number 62210]. I am appreciative to the PIs on that grant, Jim Al-Khalili and Andrea Rocco at the University of Surrey, and to fellow philosophers on the project Simon Saunders at the University of Oxford and Eddy Keming Chen at the University of San Diego for much inspiration and many valuable conversations. Work connected to this Element was presented in Oxford, Bonn, Castiglioncello and Groningen and I am grateful to the audiences at those talks for feedback. I'm also grateful to Jim Weatherall and Cambridge University Press for the opportunity to write this text, and for their help, support, and patience throughout the process. I am also appreciative to Theodor Nenu for providing the perfect complement to my mornings struggling with this Element by offering a similarly challenging afternoon on the tennis court.

Finally, thanks, as ever, to Ana-Maria Crețu for constant inspiration and support.

Cambridge Elements ≡

The Philosophy of Physics

James Owen Weatherall
University of California, Irvine

James Owen Weatherall is Chancellor's Professor in the Department of Logic and Philosophy of Science at the University of California, Irvine. He is the author, with Cailin O'Connor, of The Misinformation Age: How False Beliefs Spread (Yale, 2019), which was selected as a New York Times Editors' Choice and Recommended Reading by Scientific American. His previous books were Void: The Strange Physics of Nothing (Yale, 2016) and the New York Times bestseller The Physics of Wall Street: A Brief History of Predicting the Unpredictable (Houghton Mifflin Harcourt, 2013). He has published approximately 50 peerreviewed research articles in journals in leading physics and philosophy of science journals and has delivered over 100 invited academic talks and public lectures.

About the Series

This Cambridge Elements series provides concise and structured introductions to all the central topics in the philosophy of physics. The Elements in the series are written by distinguished senior scholars and bright junior scholars with relevant expertise, producing balanced, comprehensive coverage of multiple perspectives in the philosophy of physics.

Cambridge Elements

The Philosophy of Physics

Elements in the Series

Philosophy of Particle Physics
Porter Williams

Foundations of Statistical Mechanics
Roman Frigg and Charlotte Werndl

From Randomness and Entropy to the Arrow of Time
Lena Zuchowski

Philosophy of Physical Magnitudes
Niels C. M. Martens

The Philosophy of Symmetry
Nicholas Joshua Yii Wye Teh

Laws of Physics
Eddy Keming Chen

Foundations of General Relativity
Samuel C. Fletcher

Gauge Theory and the Geometrization of Physics
Henrique De Andrade Gomes

Causation in Physics
Christopher Gregory Weaver

Why Do We Want a Theory of Quantum Gravity?
Karen Crowther

Philosophy of Cosmology and Astrophysics
Siska De Baerdemaeker

Classical and Quantum Phase Space Mechanics
Karim Pierre Yves Thébault

A full series listing is available at: www.cambridge.org/EPPH

For EU product safety concerns, contact us at Calle de José Abascal, 56–1°, 28003 Madrid, Spain or eugpsr@cambridge.org.